MEXICAN SNACKS

★ ★ ★ ★ ★

MEXICAN SNACKS

BOTANAS, TACOS, BURRITOS, SALSAS, AND MORE!

★ ★ ★ ★ ★

MARLENA SPIELER

CHARTWELL BOOKS, INC.

A QUINTET BOOK

Published by Chartwell Books
A Division of Book Sales, Inc.
114 Northfield Avenue,
Edison, New Jersey 08837

This edition produced for sale in the U.S.A., its
territories and dependencies only.

ISBN 0-7858-0385-8

This book was designed and produced by
Quintet Publishing Limited
6 Blundell Street
London N7 9BH

Creative Director: Richard Dewing
Designer: Ian Hunt
Project Editor: Stefanie Foster
Editor: Barbara Croxford
Illustrator: Joanne Makin

Typeset in Great Britain by
Central Southern Typesetters, Eastbourne
Manufactured by C. H. Colour Scan Sdn. Bhd., Malaysia
Printed in Singapore by Star Standard Industries (Pte) Ltd

ACKNOWLEDGEMENTS

A warm thank you to those who sampled my recipes, enjoying the successes and good-naturedly putting up with the dishes that didn't quite make it. To my daughter Leah for her continual enthusiasm for the pleasures of the table, especially the Mexican table. To my step-daughter Gretchen, with whom I have shared many late-night carnitas quesadillas picnics; to my husband Alan McLaughlan for his stamina and creative shopping; to Peter Milne for his appreciation and delicious food ideas; to Jon Harford for his vegetarian sensibility in recipe testing; to Hoops and everyone at Outdoor Chef, where the grilled and barbecued dishes were tested on the marvellous gas barbecue.

Jerome Freeman and Sheila Hannon, Amanda Hamilton and Tim Hemmeter, Christine and Maureen Smith, Nigel and Graham, Esther Novack and John Chendo, Fiona Beckett, Kathleen Griffen, Sheila Dillon, Kamala Friedman, Sandy Waks, Trish Robinson, Michelle Schmidt, Simon Parkes, Michael Bauer, M.A. and Richard Mariner for the tortilla press,

Paula Levine for the tortillas, Jill Vaux, Vanessa Welch, Etty and Bruce Blackman, Paul Richardson, Susan Redgrave, Helene and Robin Simpson, the Wight family, Lena Gilbert and Jason Gaber all tucked in to various dishes and helped in the testing, even if they weren't aware of it at the time. Thanks to Jackie Higuera McMahan, for her company one lovely afternoon in San Francisco's Mission District. Thanks, too, to my lovely cat Freud, though having a cat who insists his food bowl is garnished with fresh coriander and accompanied by tortillas is as annoying as it is amusing.

Thanks to my parents, Caroline and Izzy Smith, Aunt Estelle and Uncle Sy Opper, and Grandmother Sophia Dubowsky who whetted my appetite for Mexican food when I was young and vulnerable to this delicious life-long addiction.

And to Stefanie Foster and Quintet Publishing for commissioning me to write this book.

CONTENTS

INTRODUCTION

Snacking in Mexico is a continual feast: wherever you are there is likely to be something utterly delicious on offer at a humble stall beckoning you almost irresistibly.

The marketplace abounds with stalls piled high with fruits and vegetables, straw baskets of sea creatures, the smells of roasting meats, stacks of warm tortillas and cazuelas (ceramic casseroles) filled with savory stews to wrap up in them. There are chickens revolving on spits, skewers of meats suspended over hot coals, and the everpresent patting of tortillas.

Bus stations, neighborhood corners, city parks, and town squares lure and entice passers-by with their seductive aromas. It is impossible to walk by – even if you thought you weren't hungry something will inevitably catch your eye and before you know it you are offering a handful of pesos and biting into a tiny taco, a half dozen briny fresh oysters dabbed with eye-watering salsa, a stick of juicy fruit powdered with fiery chili, or even a bowl of soup with lime and pungent green chili. Because mealtimes in Mexico are quite formalized, with a main meal eaten at midday, and a serious progression of courses, snacking is very much the opposite. It is joyfully chaotic.

At mealtimes there are rules, both social and gastronomical; the family gathers together, and the home is a cool harbor in the storm of business, school, work, and so on. And afterwards, there is usually time for a nap, to prepare for the rigors of the rest of the day.

But when snacking, there are no rules, only delight. Eat a taco at any time, walking down the street or sitting in a park, drench it with salsa and devour it in big bites by yourself or politely nibble on it with your best friend at teatime.

Mexican snacks vary from light and vivacious to solid and quite filling. You might eat walking down the street, but you might stop in at the taqueria and sit at a ceramic tiled table, downing several late-night tacos with glasses of cooling beer, while mariachis sing and strum their guitars.

Snacks are nibbled in bars and cantinas, where the owner sets out little plates of botanas (savory nibbles such as tiny tacos, pieces of browned chorizo), to encourage more drinking. You might go for a walk through a park and pass a stall that sells soup; suddenly you find yourself supping on a bowl of richly flavored consommé, sparked with chilis and splashed with lots of sour lime juice. When you have finished, you are utterly refreshed.

Fresh fruit is a quintessential Mexican snack – no surprise with their abundance of luscious tropical fruits. On streets you will find stalls with large jars of rainbow colored liquids sitting in them, sweet cooling potions of puréed fruit mixed with water and sugar (aguas de frutas). There will be blenders set up at some stalls, ready to whirl creamy drinks based on milk, rice or even masa, along with the sweet fruit.

Sometimes Mexican snacks are surprising: orange slices peppered with cayenne from the Yucatan, boiled potatoes eaten from a paper cone drenched in hot chili salsa and lime, or grasshoppers fried to a crisp crunch (*the* snack of Oaxaca).

Salsa is an intrinsic part of snacking, since a swipe of flavorful salsa turns even a plain tortilla into a near-celestial snack. Based on chilis, salsa can wake palates that have grown lethargic from the tropical heat. Salsa is endlessly varied and can range from green to red, hot to mild, fresh tasting to smoked (such as chipotle), pickled (as in escabeche). Even fruit finds its way into salsa, as the sweetness of the fruit sugar helps balance the fire of the chili.

The following collection of recipes is a gathering of some of my favorite Mexican snacks. They range from complex to very simple, and are all in the spirit of that vibrant food I never cease to enjoy either cooking or eating.

There are a few notes I wish to include: recipes are usually streamlined both in fat content and time demands already. For instance, the traditional fat of Mexican cuisine is lard. I prefer for health reasons to use vegetable and olive oil, therefore my recipes call for oil, and usually much less than traditional recipes. However, for those who wish to cut down further I offer suggestions and variations with many of the recipes. Fromage frais, for instance, is excellent on tostadas in place of sour cream; and many tortilla-based snacks or antojitos can be piled up with salady things, crunchy and fresh, and nearly free of fat or calories. To save time, chili powder is often terrific in place of steeping whole dried chilis for sauces and stews. Look at the end of each recipe for such suggestions.

GLOSSARY

CHILIS

Capsicum frutescens, otherwise known as chilis, or hot peppers, come in so wide a variety they are nearly impossible to categorize. However, there are some basic guidelines to help us with the chilis that are more easily available outside of Mexico.

> WHENEVER USING CHILIS, TAKE CARE. WASH YOUR HANDS IMMEDIATELY AFTER USING, AND DO NOT TOUCH YOUR EYES OR OTHER SENSITIVE AREAS AS THE VOLATILE OILS LINGER AND LINGER. TO PREVENT YOUR HANDS FROM BURNING FOR DAYS AFTER HANDLING CHILIS, USE RUBBER GLOVES.
>
> WHEN HEATING CHILIS IN A PAN, OR WHIRLING THEM IN A BLENDER OR FOOD PROCESSOR, DO NOT INHALE OR PLACE YOUR FACE NEAR THE LID WHEN REMOVING IT. INHALING CHILI FUMES CAN BE VERY PAINFUL AND DISTRESSING. CHILDREN ARE PARTICULARLY SUSCEPTIBLE AND SHOULD NOT BE IN THE SAME ROOM WITH FRYING CHILIS.

Chilis come fresh or dried. Fresh they are bright and full flavored, most often available in green, but red and sometimes yellow varieties are also found. Generally, with a few explosive exceptions, the smaller the chili the hotter.

Tiny Thai, or bird's eye chilis are very very hot, serranos on the hotter side of medium, while the larger Kenya, or jalapeño, are hot but not impossible. The jalapeño type chilis are probably the most useful all-purpose chili, for their pleasant flavor and bearable heat. The poblano chili looks much like an ordinary green pepper and is on the milder side as chilis go; it is lovely for stuffing. The most widely available exception to the "small is hottest" rule is the Scots bonnet, a lantern shaped chili in parrot-like hues of red, yellow, green, and orange that is breathtakingly, aggressively hot. This is one of the most readily available of chilis, and care should be taken to acclimatize yourself to its tropical heat.

Fresh green chilis may be used raw, cooked, or roasted, then added to sauces, stews, etc.

Dried chilis come in a wide range of types such as pasilla, ancho, guajillo, puya, cascabel, and so on. These are the chilis used to make "mild chili powder". To make your own mild chili powder lightly toast whichever chili you desire, then cut off stems and remove the seeds. Cut the lightly toasted chili into small pieces and whirl in a coffee grinder until it forms a powder. Storebought mild chili powder may be mixed with paprika and used in place of the individual chilis in sauces.

CHIPOTLE CHILI

This is the dried, smoked jalapeño, fiery hot and scented with smoke. It is available dried or in tins "en adobo", a spicy marinade. A recipe for chipotles en adobo is in the Salsa chapter.

JALAPEÑOS EN ESCABECHE

These pickled chilis are delicious with refried beans and cheese, or tucked into any taco or torta. Widely available.

TOMATILLOS

Green husk tomatoes with a sour flavor and a crisp texture. They must be husked and blanched before using, as raw they are not so delightful as when tender and ready to be puréed into sauces. Since they add a tart accent, occasionally unsweetened gooseberries or shredded sorrel, or a big squeeze of lemon and underripe tomatoes can take their place.

NOPALES

Cactus pads, an unusual green vegetable doted on throughout Mexico. Must be peeled and blanched first to rid them of their sticky juices (much like okra). Occasionally available fresh in West Indian markets; imported from Mexico in cans. If unavailable, use blanched green beans tossed with a few drops of vinegar, onion, and oregano.

SOME MEXICAN COOKING METHODS

ROASTING AND PEELING CHILIS

Place chilis of any sort over a flame and cook, lightly charring the skin, turning until evenly charred. If using small chilis, place them in an ungreased skillet instead or skewer them before placing on flame. When evenly and lightly charred place in a plastic bag or in the bottom of a saucepan. Seal the bag or place the lid on the pan and leave for 30–60 minutes. Remove and use a paring knife to peel off. Cut off and discard the stem and remove the seeds.

TOASTING GARLIC AND ONIONS

Place unpeeled garlic cloves in a heavy ungreased skillet and cook over medium heat until cloves char lightly and turn soft inside; turn several times so that they cook evenly. Remove from pan. To use, squeeze from skin. Use the cooked flesh and discard the skin. Onions may be toasted by cutting them unpeeled (or peeled, as desired) in half, then placing the cut pieces on an ungreased pan and cooking over medium heat until charred. Remove and use the flesh as desired.

REHYDRATING CHILIS

Lightly toast dried chilis by holding them over a flame or tossing them in a heavy ungreased pan over medium low heat. Place in a bowl and cover with boiling water. Let sit 30–45 minutes until chilis are soft, then either purée and sieve, or scrape away the flesh from the papery skin (which should then be discarded).

MASHING GARLIC

To extract full flavor from garlic, use a mortar and pestle; add a dash of salt before crushing.

ROASTING TOMATOES

Place tomatoes in a baking dish and drizzle with oil and salt. Bake in a medium hot oven for 45 minutes or until they shrink and concentrate in flavor. Let cool in their juices then remove skins and squeeze to extract the flavorful juices in the skins. Discard squeezed out skins and combine with the flesh of the tomatoes and with the pan juices. Tomatoes may also be toasted, using the technique described above for onions and garlic.

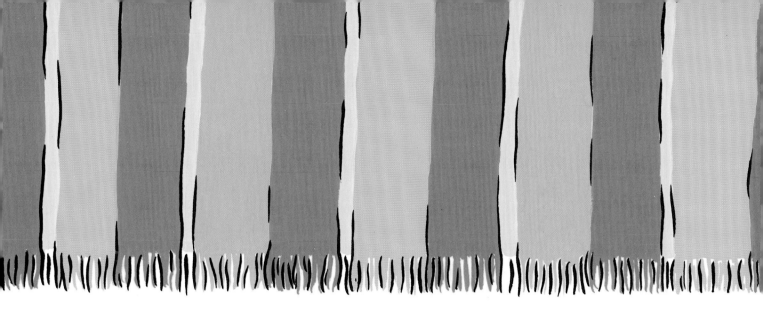

CHAPTER ONE

LA TAQUERIA

TACOS

Tacos are corn tortillas filled with nearly anything. They can be as simple as a fresh tortilla wrapped around a piece of barbecued meat or a sprig of watercress, or they can be elaborate concoctions of complex and/or elegant mixtures. You can buy them from a street vendor or at a cafe-type restaurant specializing in tacos, a taqueria.

Tacos can be soft, that is simply a tortilla wrapped around a filling. They can be crisp: either fried then filled, or fried after they are filled. Taquitos and their two-tortilla longer version, the flauta, belong to the latter category: soft tortillas wrapped around a filling, then fastened with a toothpick and fried in hot oil. When making soft tacos, it is authentic to use two small tortillas. However, since purchased tortillas are larger than homemade ones, a two-tortilla taco becomes more than just a snack. I have therefore adjusted the recipes to include one tortilla per taco. If you are making your own, and they are light and thin enough, by all means use 2 tortillas per taco.

TACOS DE CORDERO

TACOS OF SAUTEED CHILI-SEASONED LAMB, GREENS, WITH GOAT'S CHEESE

MAKES 8 TACOS

5 cloves garlic, chopped

2tbsp. mild red chili powder

2tbsp. tequila (or beer or vodka)

½tsp. ground cumin

salt to taste

juice of ½ orange

grated rind of ¼ orange

10–12oz. lamb chops, such as loin or shoulder, boned and diced

1–2tbsp. vegetable or olive oil

8 corn tortillas

5oz. soft goat's cheese

handful of greens, such as purslane or shredded lettuce

large dash oregano, crumbled

1–2 ripe tomatoes, diced

2 green onions, thinly sliced

1. Combine the garlic with the chili powder, tequila, cumin, salt, orange juice and rind, and mix well to form a paste. If it is too runny, add a little extra mild chili powder or paprika.

2. Toss the lamb in this chili paste and coat well. Let stand for at least 30 minutes.

3. Brown the lamb in a tiny amount of the oil, then set aside.

4. Warm the tortillas in a very lightly greased pan or nonstick pan with a little oil.

5. Spread the warm tortillas with the goat's cheese. Sprinkle with the oregano, then spoon on the lamb. Garnish with tomatoes, greens, and green onion. Eat right away.

NUTRITIONAL INFORMATION				
	TOTAL FAT	SAT FAT	CHOL	ENERGY
Total	95g	59g	204mg	2222kcals
Per Taco	12g	7g	26mg	278kcals

TACOS DE MOLE
SOFT TACOS OF CHICKEN AND MOLE

This is a streamlined version of mole: a savory chili sauce enlivened with a hint of chocolate and ground nuts rather than the complex feast of a true mole. It is worth making your own tortillas for this as their lovely corn taste is so much more aromatic than purchased tortillas.

MAKES 8 TACOS

2tbsp. pasilla chili powder

2tbsp. ancho chili powder

2tbsp. New Mexico or California chili powder

4¼ cups chicken stock, or as needed

2tbsp. paprika

2tbsp. peanut butter

3–4tbsp. slivered almonds

2tbsp. toasted sesame seeds

1 stale tortilla, cut into small pieces

handful of raisins

1oz. semi-sweet chocolate

3 cloves garlic, chopped

¼tsp. ground cinnamon

1 onion, chopped

2tbsp. oil

dash each oregano, cumin, and cloves

2 ripe medium tomatoes, diced

8 corn tortillas

pickled jalapeños (sliced, from a jar)

1⅓–1⅔ cups cooked shredded chicken

4–6 leaves Romaine lettuce, shredded

2–3 green onions, thinly sliced

2tbsp. chopped fresh cilantro

1. Toast the chili powder in a heavy ungreased skillet until lightly changed in color but not browned and darkened.

2. Add enough of the chicken stock to the chili to make a paste, then purée in a blender or food processor with the peanut butter, almonds, sesame seeds, tortilla, raisins, chocolate, garlic, cinnamon, and onion.

3. Heat the oil in a skillet and add this paste to the pan, stirring and cooking for about 10 minutes. Add 2 cups stock, the oregano, cumin, cloves, and tomato.

4. Simmer for about 15 minutes, adding more stock as needed, then blend in a blender or food processor once again.

5. Taste for seasoning; set aside and keep warm.

6. Warm the chicken and set aside.

7. Make the tortillas (page 74) and keep them warm in a clean cloth. Homemade tortillas can be a little thicker than purchased ones; instead of folding over or rolling up, simply serve open-faced, like a tostada, instead of a taco.

8. Smear one side with mole, pile with chicken, then garnish with lettuce, pickled jalapeño, green onion, and cilantro. Eat right away.

NUTRITIONAL INFORMATION

	TOTAL FAT	SAT FAT	CHOL	ENERGY
Total	162g	53g	140mg	3698kcals
Per Taco	20g	6.5g	17mg	462kcals

VARIATIONS
TIME SAVING

Mole freezes extremely well for about 2 months. Divide the recipe into four containers, each enough for about ½ chicken or four enchiladas or tacos. Chicken may be purchased roasted rather than cooked at home.

VEGETARIAN

Omit the chicken and make the mole with vegetable stock. Serve topped with fromage frais or sour cream.

TACOS DE TINGA

SPICY SHREDDED MEAT SOFT TACOS FROM PUEBLA

Tinga is a spicy mixture of long-simmered meat, shredded and browned, then seasoned with chipotle chilis and often with pieces of browned chorizo, in addition. It is the filling you will find most often in Puebla: in soft tacos, crispy ones, on top of tostadas, and served simply from cazuelas, to be eaten with tortillas, lettuce, and beans.

MAKES 8 TACOS

1 onion, chopped	salt, pepper, and cumin to taste
3 cloves garlic, chopped	8 corn tortillas
1 tbsp. olive or vegetable oil, or 2 slices bacon, diced	3 green onions, thinly sliced
8oz. fork-tender cooked meat (beef, pork, or lamb), shredded	5–8 radishes, diced
1 cup diced tomatoes, including their juices	2 tbsp. chopped fresh cilantro
1 tsp. marinade from canned chipotle chili en adobo or to taste	1 avocado, peeled and sliced
	½–¾ cup sour cream
	salsa of choice

1. Lightly sauté the onion and garlic in the olive or vegetable oil or bacon. Add the meat and cook until lightly browned and slightly crispy but still moist.

2. Add the tomatoes and chipotle marinade and cook down until the liquid evaporates and the mixture is dry but succulent.

3. Season with salt, pepper, and cumin.

4. Warm the tortillas, then place a spoonful of the warm meat mixture on the edge of one tortilla. Garnish with green onion, radishes, cilantro, and avocado, then garnish with a dab of sour cream and salsa of choice. Roll up and keep warm; continue filling and rolling until all the tortillas are filled, then eat right away.

VARIATIONS

Instead of soft tortillas wrapped around the filling, prepare tortillas as for tostadas, either by frying or oven crisping. Place crisp golden tortillas on a plate, one per person, and top with warm meat filling, green onions, radishes, cilantro, avocado, sour cream, and a scattering of shredded lettuce.

LOWER FAT

Cook the onions in a nonstick pan and omit all but a drop of fat from browning the meat; do the same with the tortillas. Fromage frais or yogurt may be used in place of sour cream.

TIME SAVING

Prepare a tinga using meat left over from braised meats and vegetables.

TACOS DE PESCADO CON SALSA VERDE

FISH TACOS

WITH GREEN SALSA

Fish tacos are eaten throughout Mexico, filled with whatever the generous sea has offered that day. If salsa verde is not available, serve the tacos with any other fresh, tangy salsa.

MAKES 8 TACOS

12–16oz. firm fleshed white fish, such as red snapper or cod	½ cup fish stock
salt and pepper to taste	juice of ½ lemon or lime
¼tsp. ground cumin	8 corn tortillas
¼tsp. chili powder	oil for heating tortillas
dash oregano, crumbled	Salsa Verde, as liked (page 68)
3 cloves garlic, finely chopped or minced	2tbsp. chopped fresh cilantro
	2 tbsp. chopped onion

1. Combine the fish with salt, pepper, cumin, chili, oregano, garlic, and fish stock in a saucepan. Gently bring to a boil, then immediately remove from the heat and let cool gently.

2. When cool enough to handle, break up into bite-sized pieces and season with a squeeze of lemon juice.

3. Heat the tortillas. Stack onto a plate or into a cloth-lined basket and keep covered while you finish the rest of the tortillas.

4. To assemble the tacos: gently reheat the fish, then roll up several chunks into each warm tortilla. Sprinkle with salsa, cilantro, and onion as you roll them up, then serve with extra salsa for dipping.

NUTRITIONAL INFORMATION				
	TOTAL FAT	SAT FAT	CHOL	ENERGY
Total	7g	0.5g	161mg	1355kcals
Per Taco	1g	neg	20mg	169kcals

VARIATION
TIME SAVING

Fish tacos may be prepared using leftover simmered or poached fish. Warm gently before rolling up into tacos.

NOTE

Salsa verde, or green salsa, from a jar is fine in this dish. You can enliven it with a little cumin, chopped cilantro, lime juice, and garlic or onion if needed.

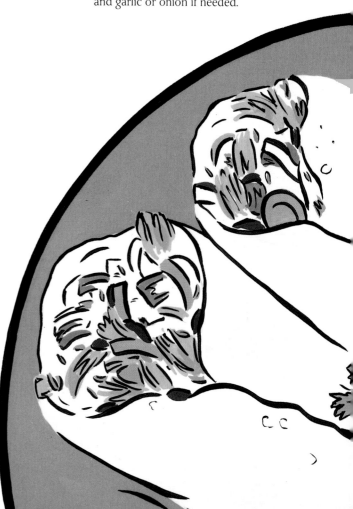

TACOS DE LANGOSTA Y FRIJOLES

LOBSTER AND BEAN TACOS

Elegant lobster pairs brilliantly with the humble bean in this taco that I once ate in a beachside restaurant on a lonely stretch of land south of Ensenada.

MAKES 8 TACOS

2 tbsp. butter	dash cumin
2 cloves garlic, chopped	8 corn tortillas
the meat from 2 lobster tails or 1 whole lobster	oil for warming tortillas
squeeze of lemon or lime	1tbsp. finely chopped fresh cilantro or parsley
2–2⅓ cups refried beans, warmed	fresh salsa of choice

1. Melt the butter with the garlic, taking care not to fry the garlic merely warm it through and release its aroma.

2. Warm the lobster in the garlic butter. Squeeze over the lemon or lime; set aside and keep warm.

3. Season the warmed beans with cumin; set aside and keep warm.

4. Warm the tortillas in lightly oiled pan. Spread each tortilla with beans, then with several spoonfuls of lobster. Sprinkle with cilantro or parsley and add salsa to taste. Roll up and serve right away.

NUTRITIONAL INFORMATION

	TOTAL FAT	SAT FAT	CHOL	ENERGY
Total	74g	25g	261mg	2242kcals
Per Taco	9g	3g	33mg	280kcals

VARIATION
LOWER FAT

Warm the tortillas in a nonstick pan with only a drop of oil. Omit the butter and warm the lobster over hot coals, basting once or twice with a little olive oil and lots of garlic.

TACOS DEL PESCADO A LA ENSENADA

ENSENADA FISH TACOS
WITH RED CABBAGE SALAD

Tacos of fish cooked over an open fire, topped with red cabbage salad, is a favorite of the Baja California town of Ensenada.

MAKES 8 TACOS

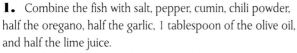

12–16oz. firm fleshed white fish, such as red snapper or cod

salt and pepper to taste

¼tsp. ground cumin

1tsp. chili powder

¼tsp. oregano, crumbled

3 cloves garlic, finely chopped or minced

2tbsp. olive oil

juice of 1½–2 limes

¼ red cabbage, thinly sliced or shredded

hot pepper sauce to taste

8 corn tortillas

½ onion, chopped

1tbsp. chopped fresh cilantro

fresh salsa of choice

1. Combine the fish with salt, pepper, cumin, chili powder, half the oregano, half the garlic, 1 tablespoon of the olive oil, and half the lime juice.

2. Broil or barbecue until just cooked through.

3. Combine the cabbage with the remaining oregano, garlic, olive oil, and lime juice. Season with salt and hot pepper sauce to taste.

4. Warm the tortillas in a lightly greased skillet or comal. Place some warm grilled fish in each tortilla, along with a big spoonful of the cabbage salad. Sprinkle with onion and cilantro, then roll up. Serve with fresh salsa of choice on the side.

NUTRITIONAL INFORMATION				
	TOTAL FAT	SAT FAT	CHOL	ENERGY
Total	29g	3.5g	161mg	1585kcals
Per Taco	3.5g	0.5g	20mg	198kcals

VARIATION
LOWER FAT

Omit the oil from both the spicy paste and cabbage salad.

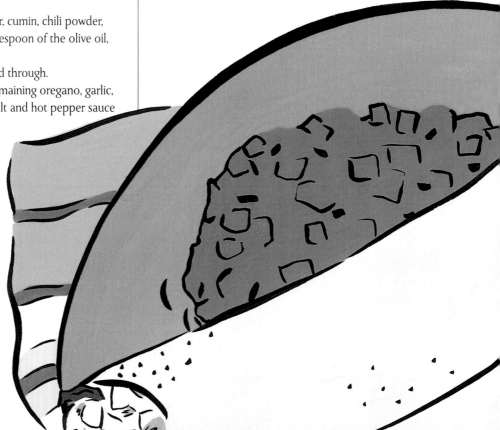

TACOS DE CAMPESINA

COUNTRYSIDE TACOS OF MARINATED AND BROWNED BEEF TONGUE

Tongue is popular in tacos all over Mexico, its smooth and firm texture and meaty taste is delicious with the other flavors of chili, tortillas, and various sauces. If tongue is not to your liking, brisket or other simmered piece of beef is delicious instead.

MAKES 8 TACOS

2 potatoes, each cut into several pieces

1 carrot, cut into pieces

handful green beans or nopale cactus

1tbsp. mild vinegar

salt and pepper

12oz. simmered tongue (or other cut of beef, such as brisket or other roast), cut into ¼–½ inch thick slices

½ onion, chopped

2 cloves garlic, chopped

1tbsp. paprika or mild chili powder, such as ancho

¼–½tsp. ground cumin

dash oregano, crumbled

1–2tsp. fruit vinegar or balsamic vinegar

1–2tbsp. adobo marinade from canned chipotle chilis

1–2tbsp. olive oil

8 corn tortillas

1. Cook the potatoes and carrot until just tender. Cook the green beans or nopales until just tender (if using canned nopales, omit this step). Let the vegetables cool, then peel and dice the potato and dice the carrot. Toss with the vinegar, salt and pepper, and set aside for the garnish.

2. Toss the tongue or other meat with the onion, garlic, paprika or mild chili powder, cumin, oregano, vinegar, marinade, and olive oil. Let marinate for 10–30 minutes.

3. Broil or pan-brown, then cut into bite-sized pieces and keep warm while you heat the tortillas.

4. Heat the tortillas then, one at a time, fill with the meat, vinegar-dressed vegetables, shredded lettuce, diced tomatoes, and salsa of your choice. Serve at once, with extra salsa as desired.

NUTRITIONAL INFORMATION				
	TOTAL FAT	SAT FAT	CHOL	ENERGY
Total	100g	2g	945mg	2359kcals
Per Taco	12.5g	0.1g	118mg	295kcals

VARIATION
TIME SAVING

Omit the garnish of cooked potato, carrot, and green beans. Use cooked tongue, bought at a delicatessen instead of cooking your own.

TACOS DE HUEVOS CON CARNITAS Y SALSA VERDE

SCRAMBLED EGG TACOS
WITH SHREDDED PORK AND GREEN SALSA

Tangy green salsa is splashed onto this deliciously rich platter of scrambled egg tacos and savory carnitas. Great for brunch or middle of the night supper, when the tequila has been flowing lavishly and the mariachis are getting ready to call it a night.

MAKES 8 TACOS

12oz. cooked, drained tomatillos	1 green onion, thinly sliced
1 onion, chopped	2tbsp. butter or as needed to scramble the eggs
2 cloves garlic, chopped	8 tortillas
½tsp. ground cumin or to taste	12oz. Carnitas (page 79), or as desired, heated through
1 fresh hot green chili, chopped or to taste	2 ripe tomatoes, diced
salt and pepper to taste	about 5 radishes, chopped
10 eggs, lightly beaten	½–1 fresh hot green chili, such as jalapeño, chopped
2tbsp. milk	3tbsp. chopped fresh cilantro

1. Purée the tomatillos with half the onion and garlic. Heat through, then season with cumin, green chili, and salt. Set aside.
2. Combine the eggs with the milk and mix well. Stir in the green onion. Scramble in the butter gently until soft curds form.
3. Warm the tortillas in a lightly oiled pan, then fill each with scrambled eggs and roll up. Keep warm while you finish rolling the tacos.
4. Surround the platter of tacos with warm carnitas, then spoon on the green salsa, with some of the tacos and meat covered with sauce, some parts uncovered.
5. Sprinkle with the diced tomatoes, radishes, chili, and cilantro. Serve immediately.

NUTRITIONAL INFORMATION

	TOTAL FAT	SAT FAT	CHOL	ENERGY
Total	112g	41g	2824mg	2874kcals
Per Taco	14g	5g	353mg	359kcals

VARIATIONS
TIME SAVING

Instead of carnitas, serve the scrambled egg tacos surrounded by crisply browned thickly sliced bacon. To brown, place in a cold pan and leave to warm slowly as the fat renders: a small amount of oil may be added to the pan to coax out the bacon fat. When the bacon is browned but not crisp, place in a baking dish in the oven at 375–400°F to keep warm and crisp while the rest of the meal is cooking. Drain on paper towels before serving.

LOWER FAT

Instead of carnitas or bacon, use lower fat turkey or chicken spicy chorizo-like sausage. Eggs can be streamlined by decreasing the amount to 4–6 eggs and adding 8oz. tofu, crushed with a fork. Season with garlic and/or chopped green onion, then cook both the egg mixture and tortillas in a nonstick pan with a few drops of oil, only for flavor. Serve tacos topped with chopped green onions, cilantro, and shredded lettuce or diced tomatoes. Diced boiled potatoes tossed with roasted red and green peppers and lots of onions could be browned in a nonstick pan with a little oil to accompany the egg tacos.

TACOS POTOSINO

TACOS FROM SAN LUIS POTOSI

These tacos are filled with my favorite ingredients: light tangy cactus, rich creamy refried beans, a spoonful of smoky fiery chipotle and a few spoonfuls of whatever spicy filling I can glean from the kitchen at any given day. Spicy shredded meat, browned chorizo, diced potatoes, shellfish, sardines, even textured soya protein or sautéed tofu; any could go into a San Luis Potosi taco (though the latter two are obviously not *authentic*!).

MAKES 8 TACOS

14–16oz. Refried Beans (page 76)

1tsp. ground cumin

1 cup diced mild white melting cheese

14–16oz. shredded beef or pork Carnitas (page 79)

8 corn tortillas

oil for warming

1–2 marinated chipotle chilis, plus a little of their marinating adobo liquid, or as desired

6oz. cooked, drained nopales (canned is fine) or green beans

1tbsp. chopped fresh cilantro

1. Warm the beans with the cumin, several tablespoons of water, and cheese. Taste for seasoning and keep warm while you prepare the other ingredients.

2. Warm your chosen filling; keep warm.

3. Heat the tortillas one at a time to make them pliable. First spray them lightly with water, then warm them in a tiny amount of oil. Stack and cover with a clean cloth while you reheat the remaining tortillas.

4. To make each taco, spread some of the warm beans across the tortilla, then a spoonful of your chosen filling. Next, add a few shreds of chipotle chili and a drop or two of the marinade, then a spoonful or two of the cactus. Sprinkle with cilantro and roll up. Eat as soon as the last taco has been rolled up, offering extra chipotle chili on the side.

NUTRITIONAL INFORMATION				
	TOTAL FAT	SAT FAT	CHOL	ENERGY
Total	98g	31g	397mg	3012kcals
Per Taco	12g	4g	50mg	376kcals

VARIATIONS

Instead of beef filling try 1 chorizo sausage browned with 1 peeled diced potato; or about 2 cups peeled cooked shrimp, lightly spiced with tomatoes, chilis, or other savory flavors.

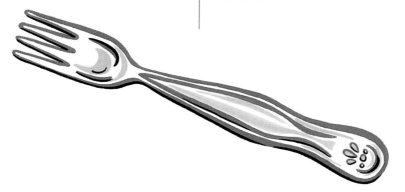

TACOS MERIDA

TACOS OF MARINATED, POACHED CHICKEN
WITH ROASTED GREEN SALSA

The marinating paste is a spice paste or recado from the Yucatan: richly red with achiote and dried red chilis, fragrant with roasted onion and garlic. I like serving them with Scorched Chili Salsa (page 69) but you can serve them with any salsa you like, tucking a few roasted green pepper strips into the tacos as you roll them up.

MAKES 8 TACOS

6 guajillo or other smooth skinned mild red chilis

1½ onions, toasted

12–15 cloves garlic, toasted

1tbsp. ground achiote (use a coffee grinder) or whole achiote seeds soaked, cooked and pounded into a paste

⅛–¼tsp. ground cinnamon

large dash cumin

large dash black pepper

small dash ground cloves

2tbsp. vinegar

⅛tsp. thyme

1tbsp. olive oil

½tsp. salt

1 tomato, chopped (canned is fine)

3 boneless half chicken breasts, cut into strips

1 cup chicken stock

juice of ¼ lime

8 tortillas

Scorched Chili Salsa (page 69) or 1 green pepper, roasted, peeled and cut into strips, with salsa of choice

lettuce, cut into strips

1. Toast the chilis over an open flame, letting them catch fire a little. Do not let them burn until they are blackened, simply let them char a little more than usual and get crisp little black edges here and there. Remove from the heat and break off the stems. Seed the chilis, then crumble the chilis into a grinder or food processor.

2. Toast onion and garlic until they are lightly charred. When cool enough to handle, dice the onion, peel the garlic, and cut up.

3. Purée the chilis with the onion, garlic, achiote, cinnamon, cumin, black pepper, cloves, vinegar, thyme, olive oil, salt, and tomato.

4. Coat the chicken strips in this paste and let marinate for 2 hours at room temperature or overnight.

5. Bring the chicken stock to a boil, then reduce the heat to low. Add the chicken, stir through gently so that it does not break up; leave to simmer for only a minute or two. They should not be cooked through. Remove from the heat and let the warmth of the pan continue to cook them so that they cook gently and do not overcook. Just before serving, drain the chicken and toss with the lime juice. (Reserve the cooking liquid and strain for soups or sauces.)

6. Warm the tortillas in a heavy lightly oiled skillet or comal.

7. Spoon several tablespoons of chicken into each warm tortilla. Spread with salsa, top with a handful of lettuce, then roll up and enjoy. Offer extra salsa or pickled jalapeños on the side.

NUTRITIONAL INFORMATION				
	TOTAL FAT	SAT FAT	CHOL	ENERGY
Total	26g	5g	129mg	1620kcals
Per Taco	3g	0.5g	16mg	203kcals

VARIATION
TIME SAVING

Omit the whole chilis and use 4 tablespoons mild red chili powder instead. Use bought achiote paste; if unavailable, add a dash of either grated orange rind or toasted saffron threads.

TACOS DE CAMARONES ASADERO
TACOS OF BARBECUED SHRIMP
FROM THE YUCATAN

MAKES 8 TACOS

6 cloves garlic, whole and unpeeled

3tbsp. ground achiote seeds (use coffee grinder)

¼ cup grapefruit juice

¼ cup orange juice

grated rind of ¼ orange

1tsp. ground cumin

1tsp. ground coriander seeds

1tsp. ground cinnamon

large dash cloves or allspice

salt and black pepper to taste

2tbsp. mild red chili powder

1tbsp. paprika

1lb. shrimp, peeled and deveined

2–3tbsp. oil

8 tortillas

salsa to taste

3tbsp. chopped fresh cilantro

Pickled Onion Rings (page 71)

1. Toast the garlic until soft and lightly charred; peel and mash. Combine with the ground achiote seeds, grapefruit and orange juice, orange rind, cumin, ground coriander, cinnamon, cloves or allspice, salt and black pepper, chili, and paprika. Toss with the shrimp and leave for 30–45 minutes.

2. Thread the shrimp onto skewers, then brush with oil. Grill over hot coals for 1–2 minutes on each side, or until the shrimp are just turning opaque.

3. Heat the tortillas and keep warm in a clean cloth.

4. When the shrimp are ready, remove from the skewers and place several into each tortilla, along with the salsa to taste and chopped cilantro. Roll up tightly and serve right away, with each taco garnished generously with pickled onions.

NUTRITIONAL INFORMATION				
	TOTAL FAT	SAT FAT	CHOL	ENERGY
Total	30g	3.5g	1260mg	1742kcals
Per Taco	4g	0.5g	158mg	218kcals

VARIATION

Strips of beef, pork, turkey, or chicken may be used in place of the shrimp.

TACOS DE RAJAS Y QUESO

SOFT TACOS OF GREEN PEPPERS, CHILIS, AND CHEESE

Rajas are simply strips of chilis; roasted, peeled, and sautéed with fragrant spicing, they make a marvelous side dish, or filling for nearly anything. Here they are simmered into a creamy cheese taco filling that tastes sublime next to the delicate corn of the tortillas.

MAKES 8-12 TACOS

2 poblano or Anaheim chilis, roasted and peeled, seeded, then cut into strips

1 green pepper, roasted, peeled, seeded and cut into strips

4 cloves garlic, chopped

2tbsp. vegetable oil

1½tsp. cumin

1tbsp. mild chili powder, such as ancho or a New Mexico blend

1tbsp. paprika

4 tomatoes, diced

2–2½ cups diced white cheese, such as Gouda, white Cheddar, etc

1 jalapeño en escabeche, chopped

½ cup sour cream

dash turmeric

dash ground ginger

juice of ½ lime or lemon

8–12 corn tortillas

1. Sauté the poblanos and green pepper with the garlic in 1 tablespoon of the oil until softened. Sprinkle with cumin for a minute or so, then stir in the chili powder, paprika, and tomatoes. Continue to cook for about 5 minutes or until tomatoes are somewhat saucelike and chunky.

2. Stir in the cheese and jalapeño en escabeche, stirring until the cheese melts, about 4–5 minutes.

3. Remove from the heat and stir in the sour cream, turmeric, and ginger. Flavor with a squeeze of lime or lemon. Set aside and keep warm.

4. Warm the tortillas either by steaming or in the remaining tablespoon of oil in a heavy pan. Spoon a tablespoon or two of the melted cheese and peppers into each warm tortilla and offer extra jalapeños en escabeche as well as extra sour cream to taste.

NUTRITIONAL INFORMATION				
	TOTAL FAT	SAT FAT	CHOL	ENERGY
Total	117g	59g	285mg	2394kcals
Per Serving (8)	15g	7g	36mg	299kcals

VARIATION
LOWER FAT

Warm the tortillas in a nonstick pan. Omit the oil for sautéeing the peppers, using a nonstick pan instead. Use a low fat cheese, and fromage frais in place of sour cream.

FLAUTAS DE CAMARONES CON SALSA DE FRUTAS

SHRIMP ROLLED CRISP-FRIED TACOS
WITH TROPICAL FRUIT SALSA

Finely chopped or minced shrimp, strongly seasoned, and rolled up into a tortilla makes a delectable taco, especially alluring when the temperature climbs really high. Try serving these flautas in a very tropical manner, piling them onto a large banana leaf, all garnished with unsprayed edible flowers such as nasturtiums.

MAKES 8 TACOS

2 cups raw peeled shrimp

1 onion, chopped

1 clove garlic, chopped

2tbsp. chopped fresh cilantro

1tsp. chipotle marinade or mild chili powder, such as ancho, or to taste

¼tsp. ground cumin

⅛tsp. thyme

large dash oregano

large dash ground cinnamon

large dash ground cloves

1 tomato, finely chopped

juice of ½ lime or to taste

salt and pepper

8 corn tortillas

oil for warming and frying tortillas

Tropical Fruit Salsa (page 66)

1. Combine the shrimp with the onion, garlic, cilantro, chipotle, cumin, thyme, oregano, cinnamon, cloves, tomato, lime juice, salt, and pepper

2. Warm the tortillas to soften. Place two tortillas next to each other, slightly overlapping. It will form a sort of oblong. Place several tablespoons of filling along the length of the tortillas, leaving a border around the edges. Roll up tightly and secure with a toothpick.

3. Fry the flautas in hot oil until lightly golden, then briefly drain on paper towels to blot any excess oil. Serve right away, each flauta garnished with a spoonful of tropical fruit salsa.

NUTRITIONAL INFORMATION				
	TOTAL FAT	SAT FAT	CHOL	ENERGY
Total	8.25g	0.5g	683mg	1542kcals
Per Taco	0.9g	neg	85mg	193kcals

VARIATIONS
TRADITIONAL

Spoon any tomato based salsa over the flautas, along with guacamole, sour cream, and chopped onions.

LOWER FAT

Instead of frying the flautas, brush the rolled filled tortillas lightly with oil. Bake in the oven at 400° until golden and crispy, about 15 minutes.

TOSTADAS

Tostadas are crisp and golden browned tortillas. Topped with a selection of varied ingredients, they are as exciting to eat as they are delicious. Each bite takes your mouth through a tour of textures: the crisp flurry of shredded lettuce or crumbling of tangy cheese, the cool billow of sour cream or the juicy nuggets of tomato, leaves of cilantro or other fragrant herbs, layers of creamy beans or finely ground meats redolent of garlic and chilis. Seafood can be spooned onto tostadas, as can goat's cheese, scrambled eggs, shredded duck, as well as beef, chicken or pork, simmered shark, braised brains, or broiled tongue.

Lately tostadas have become very chic in Mexico City, where they are centered in the plate, nouvelle cuisine style, topped and surrounded with various ingredients and sauces, drizzled on, painted on, treated like a canvas for the oh-so-delicious still life of toppings.

TOSTADAS POBLANO

PUEBLA STYLE TOSTADAS
WITH CHIPOTLE, SALSA VERDE, AND SOUR CREAM

These crisp tostadas are topped with creamy refried beans, savory meat or chicken, and both the tang of tomatillo and the fire of chipotle.

SERVES 4

8–12oz. leftover meat or chicken, diced or shredded

about 1tsp. oil, or as needed

salt, pepper, and crumbled oregano to taste

4 corn tortillas, prepared as for Tostadas (page 73)

1⅓ cups refried beans (canned is fine), warmed

⅛tsp. ground cumin

1 avocado, peeled, seeded, and sliced

Salsa Verde (page 68) (bought is fine)

1 chipotle chili, cut into strips

¾ cup sour cream

½ onion, finely chopped

handful of lettuce

5 radishes, diced

1. Warm the beef or chicken in the oil. Season with salt, pepper, and oregano; keep warm. Crisp the tostadas, then spread with refried beans and cumin.

2. Serve immediately, topped with spoonfuls of the warm meat, avocado, salsa verde, chipotle chili, sour cream, onion, lettuce, and radish.

NUTRITIONAL INFORMATION				
	TOTAL FAT	SAT FAT	CHOL	ENERGY
Total	108g	38g	278mg	2140kcals
Per Serving/ Tortilla	27g	9.5g	70mg	535kcals

VARIATIONS
TIME SAVING

Use bought ready-roasted chicken in place of home-cooked, and canned refried beans, warmed with a little water and seasonings, as well as tomatillo salsa from a jar.

LOWER FAT

Sour cream may be replaced by fromage frais. Be sure that the meat you use is trimmed of all fat. Use a nonstick pan to brown it, without the addition of extra oil or fats.

TOSTADAS DE JICARA
CAVIAR TOSTADAS

Earthy crisp tortillas topped with luxurious, briny caviar is a provocative nibble I tasted at a Mexico City artists' reception.

SERVES 4

12 small round corn tortillas, or wedges of larger corn tortillas, prepared as for Tostadas (page 73)	1 small jar black caviar
	1 small jar yellow or red caviar
¾ cup sour cream	1 small to medium onion, chopped

1. Spread the crisp tostadas with sour cream, then carefully top with black, red, and/or yellow caviar.
2. Garnish with chopped onion and serve immediately.

NUTRITIONAL INFORMATION

	TOTAL FAT	SAT FAT	CHOL	ENERGY
Total	49g	23.5g	675mg	1356kcals
Per Serving/ Tortilla	12g	6g	169mg	339kcals

TLAYUDAS
OAXACAN TOSTADAS

Tlayudas are slightly thick, very corn-flavored tortillas spread with various toppings for open tostada-like creations.

SERVES 4

4oz. cooked hominy (posole)	8oz. masa harina
¾ cup cooking liquid from hominy, or water	

1. Blend the hominy with its cooking liquid (or water), then mix with the dry masa until it forms a thick dough, much like a child's playdough.
2. Press as for ordinary tortillas (because of its consistency, tlayudas will be thicker than ordinary tortillas).
3. Cook on a hot ungreased comal or skillet. Stack and wrap in a clean tea towel to keep warm.

NUTRITIONAL INFORMATION

	TOTAL FAT	SAT FAT	CHOL	ENERGY
Total	0.5g	neg	0mg	266kcals

TLAYUDAS ROJOS
RED CHILI TLAYUDAS
WITH GREEN ONION BUTTER

SERVES 4

1 recipe Tlayuda (page 25)	½ cup butter, softened
1–2tbsp. mild chili powder, such as ancho, or to taste	3–4 green onions, thinly sliced

1. Prepare the tlayuda but add the chili powder to the dough.
2. Beat the butter together with the green onions.
3. Spread the seasoned butter over the hot tlayudas and eat immediately.

NUTRITIONAL INFORMATION

	TOTAL FAT	SAT FAT	CHOL	ENERGY
Total	83g	55g	230mg	1012kcals
Per Serving	21g	14g	58mg	253kcals

TOSTADAS DE QUESO CABRITO

GOAT'S CHEESE TOSTADAS

WITH CHILI-GARLIC STEEPED OIL

Goat's cheese has enjoyed a great revival in Mexico in recent years. Fresh and tangy, it blends deliciously with both red and green chilis, and is so light it doesn't obscure the delicacy of the other ingredients. Though cheese from goats is traditional it had fallen out of favor with commercial cheese makers from whom the predictable, plodding cow was a dependable source of milk.

Try rolling goat's cheese into enchiladas, or crumbling a spoonful into a bowl of vegetable soup along with a handful of tortillas and salsa to taste; stir goat's cheese into migas, that dish of scrambled eggs with aromatics and totopos. Or simply roll a spoonful of goat's cheese into warm corn tortillas with a spoonful of salsa verde.

This tostada is slightly more ambitious, quite elegant with its greens, yet delightfully simple and straightforward in satisfying flavor.

SERVES 4

- 1 mild red chili, such as guajillo or New Mexico, crumbled
- ¼ cup olive oil
- 1 clove garlic, cut into thin slivers
- 4 corn tortillas, prepared as for Tostadas (page 73)
- 6–8oz. goat's cheese, cut into 4 portions
- sprinkling of fresh oregano or marjoram
- handful greens, such as baby watercress, lettuce, purslane, lightly dressed with vinaigrette

1. Crumble the red chili and heat together with the olive oil gently until small bubbles form around the edge of the pan. Remove from the heat and add the garlic. Let steep until it cools, then drain. Discard the chili and garlic, or save them for sauce or soup.

2. Warm the tostadas on one side, then spread each with goat's cheese. Sprinkle with oregano, then heat briefly to warm the goat's cheese through. Serve right away, drizzled with a small amount of the red chili-garlic oil and garnished with greens.

NUTRITIONAL INFORMATION				
	TOTAL FAT	SAT FAT	CHOL	ENERGY
Total	82g	25g	0mg	1848kcals
Per Serving/ Tortilla	20g	6g	0mg	462kcals

TOSTADAS DE PATO

DUCK TOSTADAS WITH BLACK BEANS AND WILD GREENS

Another seemingly nouvelle offering that in fact goes back to traditional flavors: game meat, wild-tasting greens, and goat's or sheep's cheese. Serve with any homemade salsa for an elegant yet robust tostada.

SERVES 4

1 onion, chopped

3 cloves garlic, chopped

1–2 tbsp. olive or vegetable oil

salt and pepper to taste

½ tsp. ground cumin

3–5 tomatoes, diced (canned is fine)

meat from ½ roasted duck, cut into bite-sized pieces or shredded

large dash mild red chili powder, such as ancho or New Mexico

1 recipe Refried Black Beans (page 76), warmed

4 corn tortillas, prepared as for Tostadas (page 73)

about ¾ cup crumbled fresh cheese, such as queso fresco, fresh pecorino or a not too salty feta

handful of interesting salad greens, such as watercress, arugula, purslane etc

Chipotles en Adobo (page 70), Salsa Verde (page 68) or other fresh salsa of choice

1. Lightly sauté the onion and garlic in the oil until softened. Add salt, pepper, and cumin to taste, then stir in the tomatoes. Cook until a saucelike mixture forms. Set aside and keep warm.

2. Brown the meat lightly. Season with chili powder, salt, and pepper; keep warm.

3. Spread the black beans over the tostadas, then sprinkle with the cheese. Spoon on the meat, then the tomato mixture as required. Top with the salad greens and a spoonful of salsa. Serve right away.

NUTRITIONAL INFORMATION				
	TOTAL FAT	SAT FAT	CHOL	ENERGY
Total	118g	34g	537mg	2519kcals
Per Serving/ Tortilla	30g	8g	134mg	630kcals

TOSTADAS DE QUESO Y GUACAMOLE

FETA AND WHITE CHEESE TOSTADAS
WITH GUACAMOLE AND SOUR CREAM

This straightforward tostada of two types of cheese, mixed with garlic and oregano then melted seductively on top, served with sour cream and guacamole, tastes sumptuous and is simple to toss together.

SERVES 4

8 tortillas, lightly oiled and crisped as for Tostadas (page 73)

1 cup feta cheese, crumbled

2 cloves garlic, chopped

½ tsp. fresh oregano or to taste

1½–2 cups shredded mozzarella or Cheddar cheese

Guacamole (page 58)

¾ cup sour cream

large handful shredded Romaine lettuce, lightly tossed in vinaigrette

2–3 tbsp. sliced pickled jalapeños

1. Arrange the tostadas on a baking sheet large enough to accommodate them (or use two).

2. Sprinkle with feta, garlic, and oregano, then with shredded mozzarella or Cheddar. Broil until the cheese melts.

3. Serve each tostada garnished with guacamole, sour cream, and pickled jalapeños.

NUTRITIONAL INFORMATION				
	TOTAL FAT	SAT FAT	CHOL	ENERGY
Total	118g	63g	290mg	2399kcals
Per Serving/ Tortilla	15g	8g	36mg	300kcals

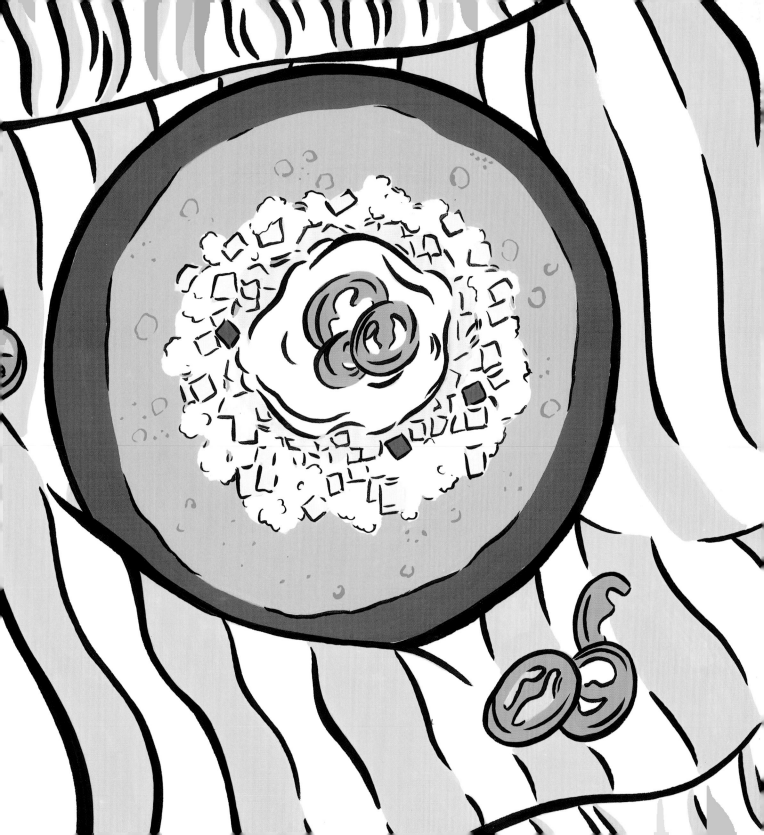

CHEESE TACOS

Simplified, quesadillas are cheese tacos. They may be little more than corn tortillas filled with cheese, then heated until it melts, or it might be fresh masa dough wrapped around cheese, then pan-browned to make a crisp cheese turnover. Quesadillas may also be made using flour tortillas. In addition to cheese, quesadillas can have any number of ingredients: salsa, chilis, sautéed meats such as brains, carnitas, or broiled meats, or savory sautéed wild mushrooms or greens.

QUESADILLA DE CHORIZO Y ALCACHOFA

CHORIZO AND ARTICHOKE HEART QUESADILLAS

This might sound an unlikely combination, but it is a delicious variation of a cactus bud quesadilla that I have sampled. Frozen artichoke hearts are fine if fresh are not available or are too time consuming; canned artichoke hearts are acceptable if rinsed well of their canning liquid.

SERVES 4

1 chorizo, about 6oz., skin removed, meat broken up

2 artichokes, trimmed of their spiky leaves and chokes, blanched until just tender (or use about 8 artichoke hearts), then diced

2 cloves garlic, chopped

4 large flour tortillas

12oz. mild white cheese

1 tomato, diced

2 green onions, thinly sliced

1tbsp. chopped fresh cilantro

hot pepper seasoning to taste (such as Habanero or Bufala Chipotle Salsa)

1. Brown the chorizo in a dry skillet, breaking it up as it cooks. Remove from the heat. Toss the artichokes with half the garlic.

2. Warm the tortillas so that they are pliable. Working one at a time, sprinkle each tortilla with chorizo, artichoke, and cheese. Fold up to enclose the filling.

3. Heat in a lightly greased skillet, until golden flecked and the cheese has melted.

4. Combine the tomato, green onions, remaining garlic, and the cilantro. Season with hot pepper seasoning and serve a spoonful with each quesadilla.

NUTRITIONAL INFORMATION				
	TOTAL FAT	SAT FAT	CHOL	ENERGY
Total	98g	59g	288mg	2068kcals
Per Serving	25g	15g	72mg	517kcals

VARIATION
LOWER FAT

Use a lower fat chicken or turkey chorizo or chilied sausage in place of the chorizo and use low fat cheese in place of full fat. Instead of rolling up the quesadilla and pan-browning, simply place the cheese side up under the broiler and melt the cheese.

QUESADILLA CON CHILE VERDE Y
QUESO FRESCO DE CABRITA

GOAT'S CHEESE AND GREEN CHILI QUESADILLAS

If your chilis are terribly piquant, place in the freezer overnight or for longer. Their heat should be somewhat mitigated when thawed. Green pepper, combined with a little smaller chili, may be used in place of the larger mild chilis.

SERVES 4

1–2 mild green chilis (depending on heat of the chilis, 1 green pepper can substitute for one of the chilis), such as Anaheim or poblano, roasted, peeled, seeded and sliced

1 clove garlic, chopped

2tsp. chopped fresh cilantro

1tbsp. olive oil

1tsp. vinegar

dash oregano

4 corn tortillas

5oz. goat's cheese, cut into slices or crumbled

1½ cups shredded mild cheese

1. Combine the chilis with the garlic, cilantro, oil, vinegar, and oregano. Let marinate for at least 30 minutes; overnight is even better.

2. Warm the tortillas in a lightly greased heavy skillet until pliable. Spoon the peppers onto the tortillas, then top with the goat's and mild cheeses. Fold over.

3. Heat the quesadillas in a heavy ungreased skillet or comal until lightly browned in spots on each side and the cheese has melted. Serve immediately.

NUTRITIONAL INFORMATION				
	TOTAL FAT	SAT FAT	CHOL	ENERGY
Total	72g	41g	123mg	1362kcals
Per Serving	18g	10g	31mg	341kcals

VARIATION
TIME SAVING

Omit the roasted and marinated green chili and instead use pickled jalapeños to taste. Combine with the cheeses and fill the tortillas, then warm in the comal or ungreased skillet.

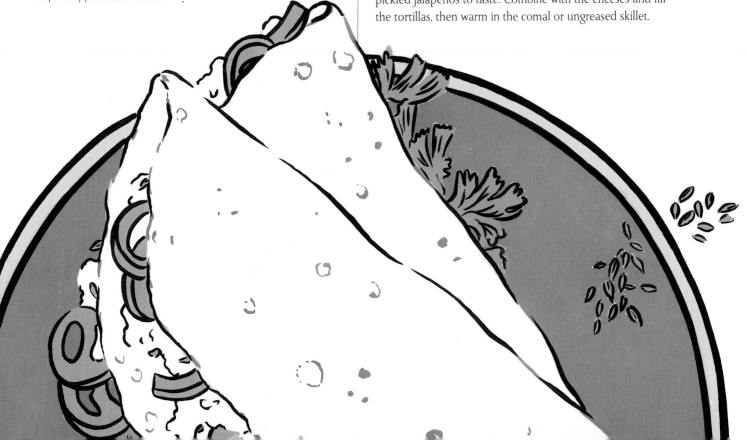

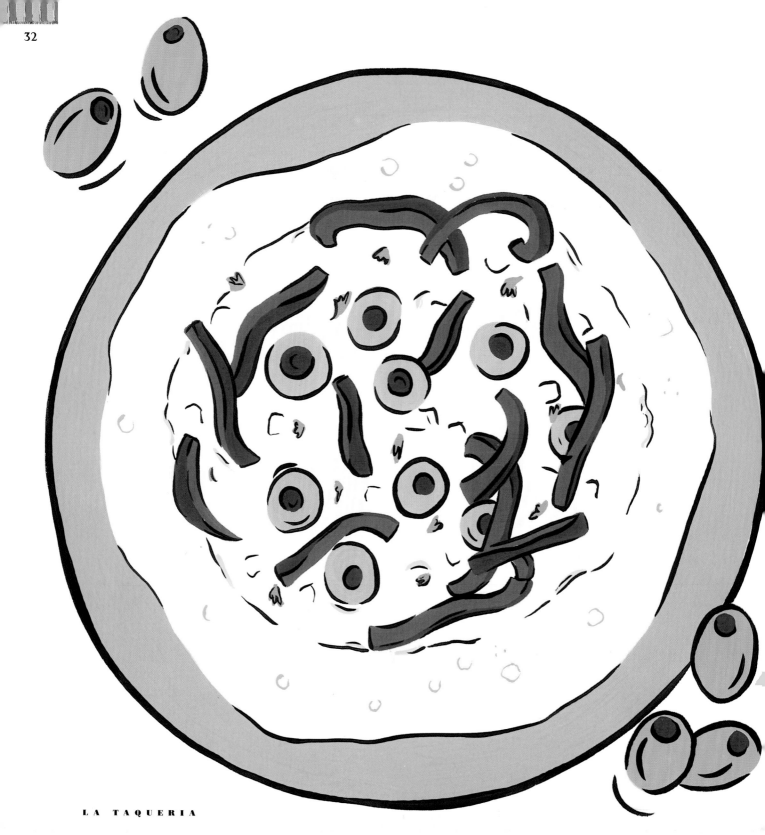

CHEESE-TOPPED FLOUR TORTILLAS
WITH GREEN OLIVE AND ROASTED RED PEPPER TOPPING

This is a simple to make yet utterly delicious quesadilla. Marvelous for an any time, any weather, snack.

SERVES 4

4 flour tortillas

2–3 cups coarsely shredded flavorful white cheese, such as white Cheddar, mozzarella, fontina, asiago, etc

about 12 pimento-stuffed green olives, sliced

1 red pepper, roasted, peeled, and cut into strips (from a jar is fine)

1–2 cloves garlic, chopped

2tbsp. chopped fresh cilantro

hot chili sauce or salsa of choice

1. Arrange the tortillas on a baking sheet.
2. Combine the cheese with the olives, red pepper, garlic, and cilantro. Divide equally and make a layer on each tortilla.
3. Sprinkle with hot sauce to taste. Broil until the cheese is melted and lightly browned in spots.
4. Serve immediately, with extra hot sauce if liked.

NUTRITIONAL INFORMATION				
	TOTAL FAT	SAT FAT	CHOL	ENERGY
Total	58g	31g	146mg	1595kcals
Per Serving	14.5g	8g	37mg	399kcals

MUSHROOM QUESADILLA IN A FLOUR TORTILLA

In Mexico, the mushroom season is a parade through a rich, fungal wonderland: little brown mushrooms known as clavitos; huitlacoche, the delectable fungus that grows on corn; yemas, with their orange-yellow hue and delicate flavor; enchilados, colored the hue of the red chili; tecamaniles, earthy in color and flavor; in addition to the mushrooms that Europeans and North Americans are more used to, morels and cèpes, as well as cultivated mushrooms.

I have prepared the following with an assortment of fresh mushrooms: shiitake, portobello, chanterelles, trompette de morte, and cèpes. They are also good using a combination of dried (soaked and rehydrated) mushrooms in addition to cultivated ones.

SERVES 4

2 cups mushrooms, thinly sliced (see above)

2tbsp. butter, plus a little extra if needed

2 cloves garlic, chopped

salt and pepper to taste

4 large flour tortillas

about 1½ cups thinly sliced or shredded mild cheese

2tbsp. chopped fresh cilantro

1 recipe Salsa Cruda (page 65)

1. Sauté the mushrooms in the butter until lightly browned. Add the garlic, salt and pepper, then remove from the heat.
2. Warm the tortillas to make them pliable. Working one at a time, sprinkle each with cheese, cilantro, salsa, and mushrooms. Fold over to enclose the filling.
3. Heat the tortillas in a hot lightly greased pan or under the broiler until the cheese melts. Serve immediately, with extra salsa if liked.

NUTRITIONAL INFORMATION				
	TOTAL FAT	SAT FAT	CHOL	ENERGY
Total	60g	37g	171mg	1249kcals
Per Serving	15g	9g	43mg	312kcals

QUESADILLA CON FRIJOLES NEGROS

BLACK BEAN AND WATERCRESS QUESADILLAS

WITH CHIPOTLE CHILI

Black beans, smoky chipotle and fresh watercress make these elegant though still earthy quesadillas.

SERVES 4

1⅓ cups cooked black beans, either well spiced with garlic, onions, tomatoes and mild red chili, or refried

2tsp. marinade from canned chipotles or chipotle salsa

3–4 ripe tomatoes, chopped

2 green onions, thinly sliced

4 large flour tortillas (12 inch)

3–4 cups shredded white cheese, such as mozzarella or white Cheddar

½ cup sour cream

handful of watercress, coarsely chopped

1. Warm the beans with a few tablespoons of water so that they heat evenly and do not burn.

2. Meanwhile, combine the chipotle marinade with the tomatoes and green onions.

3. Warm the tortillas to make them pliable. Spread them with a layer of beans and a generous sprinkling of cheese. Put on a spoonful of the tomato-chipotle mixture and fold into an envelope-like package.

4. Heat the tortillas in an ungreased pan, covered, or in a steamer, until the quesadilla is heated through and the cheese has melted.

5. Serve garnished with sour cream and watercress.

NUTRITIONAL INFORMATION				
	TOTAL FAT	SAT FAT	CHOL	ENERGY
Total	72g	41g	123mg	1362kcals
Per Serving	18g	10g	31mg	341kcals

VARIATION
LOWER FAT

Use low fat cheese in place of full fat, and fromage frais in place of sour cream.

BURRITOS

FLOUR-WRAPPED PARCELS

Burritos are flour tortillas filled with warm beans, savory meats, poultry or fish, sometimes rice and/or cheese, then splashed with salsa and wrapped tightly. They are huge and unwieldy to eat, and are one of the most appetizing of dishes one can conjure up when hungry.

Any kind of beans may be used: simmered pinto or black, or refried beans. Be sure they are warm. Guacamole and sour cream may be tucked inside, as can extra salsa, chilis, and handfuls of herbs. Wet burritos are basic burritos splashed with Mild Red Chili Sauce (page 78), then sprinkled with cheese and baked until hot and bubbly. Chimichangas are burritos that are fried in hot oil until golden.

BURRITOS DE FRIJOLES NEGROS Y MOLE

BLACK BEAN BURRITOS

WITH MOLE AND ORANGE SALSA

The fruity-spicy quality of orange salsa enhances the slightly sweet mole sauce. This is a lovely vegetarian burrito, but could include any savory braised meat, too, if liked.

SERVES 4

1 orange or 2 smaller citrus fruits, such as mandarin or satsuma, peeled, seeded and diced, including their juices and a little grated rind

1 tomato, preferably slightly unripe, diced

1 green onion, thinly sliced

¼ onion, chopped

juice of ½ lime

½tsp. sugar

1tsp. hot pepper sauce from a bottle, or to taste

4 flour tortillas

1 recipe Mole from Tacos de Mole recipe (page 11)

1 cup hot stock

1 recipe Refried Black Beans (page 76)

sour cream or fromage frais

4–5 leaves Romaine lettuce, shredded or thinly sliced

3tbsp. chopped fresh cilantro

1. Combine the orange, tomato, green onion, onion, lime juice, sugar, and hot pepper sauce. Set aside.

2. Warm the tortillas. Simmer the mole with the stock until thickened. Working one at a time, spread a generous amount of warm beans along the center of the tortilla, then spread generously with mole sauce.

3. Roll up, sealing in the edges first to enclose the filling, then keep warm while you finish the rest of the burritos.

4. Serve each burrito topped with sour cream or fromage frais, and a spoonful of the orange and tomato salsa. Sprinkle with lettuce and cilantro and eat immediately.

NUTRITIONAL INFORMATION				
	TOTAL FAT	SAT FAT	CHOL	ENERGY
Total	129g	20g	2mg	2971kcals
Per Serving	32g	5g	1mg	743kcals

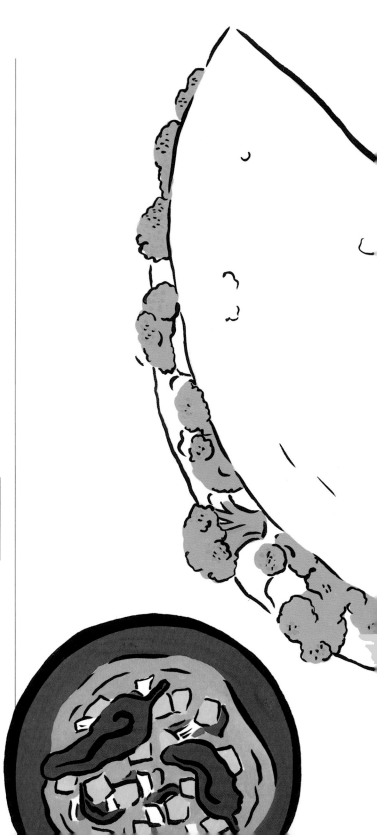

BURRITOS DE VERDERAS

BROCCOLI BURRITOS

SERVES 4

2 cups diced broccoli

¼ cup ricotta cheese, cottage cheese, or fromage frais

1 clove garlic, chopped

½tsp. ground cumin

1–1½ cups shredded Cheddar or asiago cheese

1 egg, lightly beaten

4 flour tortillas

1tbsp. vegetable oil

Chipotles en Adobo (page 70) or bought, or guajillo salsa, warmed

1. Cook the broccoli in boiling salted water until al dente, then drain. Mix with the ricotta or cottage cheese, garlic, cumin, cheese, and egg.

2. Warm the tortillas in the oil until softened and pliable. Fill with the broccoli-cheese mixture, then fold over. Heat in the pan until the cheese melts and the outside of the tortilla is lightly browned in spots.

3. Serve right away, with either the chipotle salsa or the warmed salsa guajillo. Garnish with chopped onion, chopped fresh cilantro, and diced tomatoes if liked.

NUTRITIONAL INFORMATION

	TOTAL FAT	SAT FAT	CHOL	ENERGY
Total	62g	29g	363mg	1271kcals
Per Serving	15g	7g	91mg	318kcals

VARIATION
WET BURRITOS

These burritos are particularly suited for making into wet burritos. Arrange one per person in a baking dish, then pour over about 1¾–2 cups mild chili sauce (using guajillo if liked). Sprinkle with cheese, cover with foil, then bake in the oven at 375–400° until heated through. Serve right away, with extra salsa on the side.

BURRITOS DE FRIJOLES NEGROS Y CARNE DE RES

BLACK BEAN AND BRAISED BEEF BURRITOS

WITH CHIPOTLE SALSA

Any tender, savory beef is delicious in these burritos: use leftover braised beef, barbecued steak or prepare sautéed strips of steak, or even good quality lean ground beef.

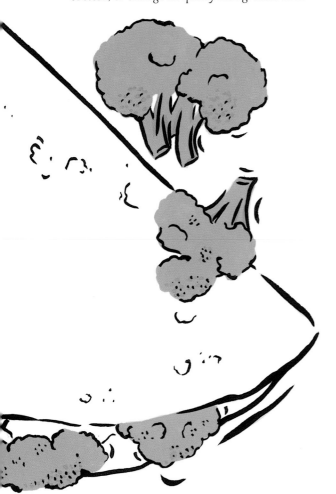

SERVES 4

½ chili chipotle en adobo, chopped in 1–2tsp. of the marinade

3–4 ripe tomatoes, diced, or canned, chopped

1 onion, chopped

1 clove garlic, chopped

1tbsp. chopped fresh cilantro

12oz. leftover chili-braised beef, shredded, or sautéed strips of chili seasoned beef (or use one of the fillings from page 79)

1 recipe Refried Black Beans (see page 76)

4 flour tortillas

about 2tsp. oil

1. Combine the chili with the tomatoes, onion, garlic, and cilantro. Set aside.

2. Shred or thinly slice the meat and warm, with a little of its flavorful braising liquid or sauce. Keep warm while you prepare the rest of the dish.

3. Warm the beans and keep warm while you heat the tortillas and assemble the dish.

4. Warm the tortillas in a little oil until pliable; fill with several spoonfuls of braised meat, warm beans, and chipotle chili tomato mixture. Roll up to enclose the filling.

NUTRITIONAL INFORMATION				
	TOTAL FAT	SAT FAT	CHOL	ENERGY
Total	128g	39g	236mg	2528kcals
Per Serving	32g	10g	59mg	632kcals

VARIATIONS
LOWER FAT

Omit the meat and fill only with beans. Use fat-free flour tortillas and serve with lots of salad and a squeeze of lime.

VEGETARIAN

Black Bean and Corn Burritos with Chipotle Salsa: In place of the beef, spoon chili-sautéed corn into the tortillas with the beans and chipotle salsa. Add shredded cheese and roll up.

To make chili-sautéed corn: Sauté cooked corn kernels with chopped onion, garlic, cumin to taste, and either a generous shake of mild chili powder, or a few spoonfuls of Mild Red Chili Sauce (page 78), salt, and pepper to taste.

BURRITOS DE CHILORIO

PORK AND RED CHILI BURRITOS

The pork filling cooked with ancho chili paste is good not only in burritos, but in tacos, tostadas, tortas, and tamales as well.

SERVES 4

2lb. pork shoulder cut into 1–2 inch cubes	salt and pepper to taste
5 ancho chilis	4 large flour tortillas
8 cloves garlic, chopped	Frijoles de Olla (simmered pinto beans, warmed and drained) (page 77)
¼tsp. oregano, crumbled	
½tsp. ground cumin	4tbsp. chopped onion
⅓ cup stock	salsa to taste
juice of ½ lime	Guacamole (page 58)

1. Cover the pork with water and simmer over a low heat for 1 hour or until the water has evaporated and meat has lightly browned.

2. Remove from the pan and shred with a fork, tossing with any juices. Set aside.

3. Lightly toast the chilis, then remove the stems, seeds, and veins. Break or cut up into small pieces, then place in saucepan with boiling water to cover. Simmer for 15–20 minutes or until they plump up.

4. In a blender or food processor, combine the chilis, garlic, oregano, cumin, stock, and lime juice until it forms a smooth paste.

5. Heat the meat in its juices and pan drippings, then add the sauce and mix well. Simmer over a low heat for about 20 minutes or until the meat has absorbed the chili sauce. Season with salt and pepper, and adjust the cumin and oregano to taste.

6. Warm the tortillas. Into each one, spoon a generous portion of meat, a ladle of beans, then a sprinkling of onion, and salsa to taste. Roll up tightly and serve right away, while still hot. Accompany with guacamole and extra salsa.

NUTRITIONAL INFORMATION				
	TOTAL FAT	SAT FAT	CHOL	ENERGY
Total	123g	39g	735mg	4293kcals
Per Serving	31g	10g	184mg	1073kcals

VARIATIONS
TIME SAVING

Use 3tbsp. mild chili powder mixed with 1tbsp. paprika in place of the whole chilis.

CHIMICHANGAS

These are a specialty of the regions that straddle the U.S./Mexican border along Arizona. Though any burrito can be turned into a chimichanga, this meaty one is particularly nice. Prepare burritos, folding carefully so that all of the filling is well wrapped. Secure each with a toothpick. Fry burrito/chimichangas in 1 inch hot oil until browned on both sides. Drain on paper towels and serve with salsa of choice, guacamole, sour cream, and chopped green onion or cilantro.

LOWER FAT

Use a simmered meat mixture instead of the one in the above recipe. Shred and season with cumin and mild chili powder. Brown with 1 chopped onion and several cloves of chopped garlic in a nonstick pan with a little oil. Instead of frying burrito/chimichangas, brush the outside of each package lightly with oil, then bake in the oven at 375–400°F long enough to heat through, about 15 minutes. Serve immediately with fromage frais or goat's cheese crumbled over the top, shredded lettuce and diced tomatoes, and salsa of choice.

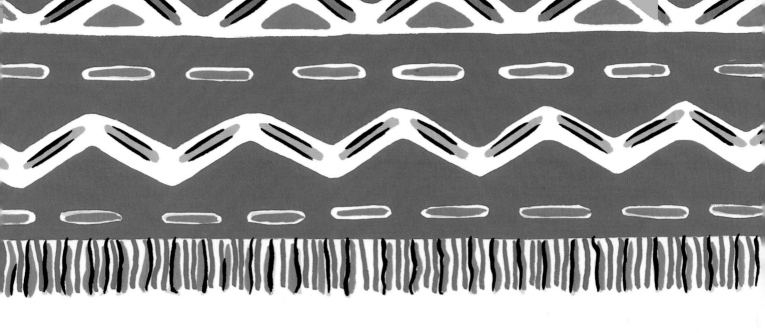

CHAPTER TWO

STREET FOODS
AND MARISCOS

★ ★ ★ ★ ★

PLUMP SANDWICHES OF TOASTED ROLLS FILLED WITH VARIED MIXTURES

Walk down the streets of any Mexican town and you will see the signs for tortas, or sandwiches. Often the word is simply scrawled on the outside of a shop window, or the side of the shop front. Sometimes it is a wooden sign saying no more.
Filled with anything from mashed beans and sardines to chorizo and salad, and/or melted cheese and ham, they are crisp-crusted, hot and satisfying.

MOLLETES

TORTAS FILLED WITH REFRIED PINTO BEANS

AND TANGY CABBAGE SALAD

Molletes are crusty rolls stuffed with hot melted beans and cheese, then garnished with a tangy, hot condiment such as pickled jalapeños. These molletes are more deluxe however: the beans are enriched with browned bacon and/or spicy chorizo, tomatoes and spices, then topped with crunchy cabbage salad.

SERVES 4

4 rolls, cut in halves and slightly hollowed out	½tsp. ground cumin or to taste
vegetable oil or bacon fat	½ cabbage, thinly sliced
1 onion, chopped	about 2tbsp. sliced pickled jalapeños, plus a little of the pickling liquid
3 cloves garlic, chopped	1tbsp. olive oil
3 slices bacon, chopped, or 2 chorizos, cut up	3tbsp. white wine or cider vinegar
8 ripe tomatoes (1lb.), peeled and chopped	salt and pepper
1 recipe Refried Beans (page 76), or use canned, warmed with a little water	crumbled oregano to taste
	2½ cups shredded white cheese

1. Preheat the oven to 400°. Brush the hollowed out rolls with oil or bacon fat. Toast in the oven until crisp and lightly golden brown.

2. Meanwhile, sauté the onion, garlic, and bacon or chorizo until the onion is softened. Add the tomatoes and cook until saucy.

3. Add the beans and stir through so that they combine with the onion, tomatoes, etc. Season with cumin and set aside; keep warm.

4. Combine the cabbage with the jalapeños, olive oil, and vinegar. Season with salt, pepper, and crumbled oregano.

5. Fill the rolls with the warm bean mixture then top with the cheese. Close up and warm through in oven. Open and fill with the cabbage salad. Serve immediately.

NUTRITIONAL INFORMATION				
	TOTAL FAT	SAT FAT	CHOL	ENERGY
Total	164g	63g	277mg	2956kcals
Per Serving	41g	16g	69mg	739kcals

VARIATION
TIME SAVING

Simply warm already prepared refried beans (homemade or canned); season with chili powder and cumin. Pile into lightly toasted hollowed out rolls, top with cheese and melt. Serve with pickled jalapeños, chopped onions, and sour cream.

TORTAS DE SARDINAS Y CHORIZO

ROLLS STUFFED WITH SARDINES AND CHORIZO

Crusty rolls are hollowed out and filled with a mixture of mashed sardines, browned chorizo, crisp raw onion, and tangy pickled jalapeños. What makes these different is that they are left overnight for the juices to soak into the bread. Just before serving, toast until crisp and lightly golden brown. Bite into it for a delicious contrast of tastes and textures.

Sardines, by the way, are often mashed and combined with chorizo for all sorts of snacks and fillings: tostadas and tacos in addition to tortas.

SERVES 4

2 chorizo sausages, about 12oz. in total, skinned and broken up

½ can sardines, mashed with a fork

½tsp. oregano, crumbled, or more to taste

4–6tbsp. sliced pickled jalapeños or more, to taste, plus a little of the pickling liquid

4 medium rolls or 8 small rolls, cut in halves and slightly hollowed out

little olive oil for brushing onto the rolls

1. Brown the chorizo until it cooks into a savory mashed mixture. Remove from the heat and let cool.

2. Mix with the onion, sardines, oregano, and jalapeños plus a little of the liquid.

3. Stuff the mixture into the rolls, then close and squeeze tightly. Place the rolls into a plastic bag and refrigerate overnight to let the juices soak into the bread.

4. Preheat the oven to 425°. Brush the outside of the rolls with oil. Bake in the oven or brown in a heavy pan, tossing and turning occasionally, until the rolls are golden brown on the outside and heated through inside.

5. Serve hot, right away, with extra jalapeños en escabeche if liked.

NUTRITIONAL INFORMATION				
	TOTAL FAT	SAT FAT	CHOL	ENERGY
Total	102g	40g	216mg	1720kcals
Per Serving	25g	10g	54mg	430kcals

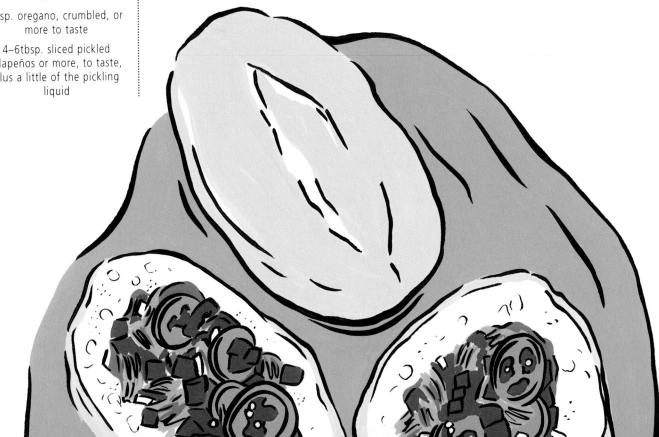

TORTA DEL MERCADO

MARKETPLACE TORTAS

I ate this torta one day in a Michoacan marketplace; the meat itself was very savory and deliciously flavored. This is especially good with any highly flavored not too lean leftover roast.

SERVES 4

about 2 cups diced cooked tender pork	3tbsp. chopped jicama, peeled and diced
2 onions, chopped	3 tomatoes, diced
3 cloves garlic, chopped	2–3 pickled jalapeño chilis, chopped
1tbsp. oil	1tbsp. chopped fresh cilantro
salt and pepper	juice of ½ lime
mild chili powder, such as New Mexico or guajillo, to taste	4 rolls
large dash marjoram	about 3tbsp. sour cream

1. Brown the meat and half the onion with the garlic in the oil. Season with salt, pepper, chili powder, and marjoram.

2. Combine the jicama, tomatoes, jalapeños, cilantro, and remaining onion with the lime juice. Season with salt and pepper.

3. Hollow out the rolls and lightly toast. Smear the insides with the sour cream.

4. Combine the hot meat with salsa and spoon into the rolls. Serve immediately.

NUTRITIONAL INFORMATION				
	TOTAL FAT	SAT FAT	CHOL	ENERGY
Total	48g	18g	412mg	1398kcals
Per Serving	12g	4g	103mg	350kcals

VARIATION
LOWER FAT

Fromage frais can be used in place of the sour cream. Turkey thigh makes a good substitute for the pork, although much of the pork available these days is lean if trimmed well.

BASIC GARNACHAS

Garnachas, gorditas (little fat ones) and chalupas (boats) are all little cuplike containers based on masa harina, which are filled with various savory fillings and crunchy salads, tostada-like.

They can be quite small and appetizer size; they might be served in a bar, at a makeshift stall on a street corner, or in a restaurant heaped onto a platter in a dazzling assortment, to be nibbled on greedily with drinks before the rest of the meal.

8oz. masa harina	1 cup cold water
3tbsp. olive oil	vegetable oil, as needed
½tsp. salt	

1. Combine the masa harina with the olive oil and salt, and work in well.

2. Stir in the cold water, working the dough until it forms a smooth pliable but not too sticky dough.

3. Roll into eight balls for garnachas or gorditas, four balls for chalupas. Flatten each and using your fingers mold a little lip around each edge.

4. Fry in hot oil until golden, then drain on paper towels. To reheat, place on baking sheet in the oven at 375–400° until crisp edged and warm through.

NUTRITIONAL INFORMATION				
	TOTAL FAT	SAT FAT	CHOL	ENERGY
Total	36g	5g	0mg	1064kcals

VARIATION
LOWER FAT

I like this way of making garnachas better than the traditional, which can be very heavy. These are lighter; crisp on the outside, corn tasting and tender inside. Place the little masa shapes on an oiled baking sheet and bake in the oven at 400° for about 15–20 minutes. The edges should brown a little and the little shapes should not fall apart when lifted off the sheet with a spatula. They will not, however, turn as golden as the fried ones do.

GARNACHAS GUADALAJARA

GARNACHAS WITH CHORIZO, POTATO, CARROT, AND NOPALES

SERVES 4

1 large potato

½ carrot, diced

1tsp. vinegar

2 chorizo sausage, 12oz., casing removed, skinned and cut into small pieces

1 onion, chopped

1 clove garlic, chopped

1 tomato, diced

3oz. nopale cactus, cooked and drained (or green beans, cut into bite-sized pieces)

dash oregano

dash ground cinnamon

dash ground cumin

1 recipe Basic Garnachas shapes (page 42)

¾ cup sour cream

Pickled Onion Rings (page 71)

1tbsp. chopped fresh cilantro

1. Part-boil the potato until almost but not quite tender. Add the carrot toward the end of cooking and cook with the potato. Remove the carrot and let cool. Rinse the potato and cool. Peel, dice and sprinkle with vinegar, then set aside.

2. Brown the chorizo in a skillet over medium heat. Add the onion, garlic, and tomato when chorizo is half cooked through. Add the potato, carrot, and nopale or green beans. Season with oregano, cinnamon, cumin, and chipotle. Warm through together, then set aside and keep warm.

3. Heap each garnacha with several spoonfuls of filling, then top with a dollop of sour cream, a sprinkling of both pickled onions and cilantro. Serve right away, with extra chipotle or pickled jalapeños on the side.

NUTRITIONAL INFORMATION				
	TOTAL FAT	SAT FAT	CHOL	ENERGY
Total	192g	67g	245mg	3691kcals
Per Serving	48g	17g	61mg	923kcals

GARNACHAS OAXAQUENO

MASA CUPS FILLED WITH REFRIED BEANS, SAVORY PORK

AND TANGY CABBAGE SALAD

These garnachas are filled with refried beans, carnitas, and a tangy raw cabbage and carrot salad.

SERVES 4

¼ cabbage

1tbsp. olive oil

2tbsp. lime juice

2 cloves garlic, chopped

1 carrot, shredded

salt to taste

dash thyme

hot pepper sauce from a bottle to taste

8 Garnachas (page 42)

1 recipe Refried Beans (page 76), warmed

1 recipe Carnitas or other meat (page 79), chopped and browned in a pan, warmed

½ onion, chopped

1. Combine the cabbage with the olive oil, lime juice, garlic, carrot, salt, thyme, and hot pepper sauce to taste.

2. Preheat the oven to 400°. Heat the garnachas on a baking sheet in the oven for about 5–8 minutes.

3. Fill the little masa shapes with warm refried beans, then top with browned meat, chopped onion, and the cabbage salad. Serve immediately.

NUTRITIONAL INFORMATION				
	TOTAL FAT	SAT FAT	CHOL	ENERGY
Total	190g	39g	635mg	4635kcals
Per Serving	47.5g	10g	158mg	1159kcals

VARIATION
LOWER FAT

Omit the olive oil from the cabbage-carrot salad and take care that the meat you use is well drained of any fat.

YUCATECAN SNACKS OF MASA AND BEANS TOPPED WITH MEAT
AND CRUNCHY VEGETABLE SALAD

This snack of black bean-enriched tortillas, fried to a crisp and topped with a variety of savory toppings, is the most often found snack in the Yucatan.

SERVES 4

8oz. masa harina	Pickled Onion Rings (page 71)
2tbsp. all-purpose flour	¼ cabbage, thinly sliced
½tsp. salt	1–2 fairly mild green or yellow chilis, seeded and chopped
2–3tbsp. black beans, puréed and thinned with a little of the cooking liquid	1–2 ripe tomatoes, chopped
4tbsp. water or black bean cooking liquid	handful of toasted pumpkin seeds
oil for frying	dash oregano, crushed
8–12oz. chili-flavored cooked pork, beef, or chicken (see any recipe for tacos, Tostadas on page 73)	

1. Mix the masa with the flour and salt, then add the beans and enough of the water or bean liquid to make a stiff dough. Let stand for 5–10 minutes.

2. Roll the mixture into 1 inch balls and flatten into 4 inch rounds. Cook each tortilla on a hot ungreased skillet or comal, stacking them as they cook.

3. Heat the oil to a depth of about 1 inch, then fry each tortilla in hot oil until crisp. Drain on paper towels.

4. Top each hot crisp tortilla with meat or chicken, pickled onion, cabbage, chilis, tomatoes, pumpkin seeds, and oregano. Eat immediately.

NUTRITIONAL INFORMATION				
	TOTAL FAT	SAT FAT	CHOL	ENERGY
Total	25g	5.75g	171mg	1611kcals
Per Serving	6g	1.5g	43mg	402kcals

MASA BOATS FILLED WITH BARBECUED MEAT, BLACK BEANS, AND CHORIZO

A good snack to remember when you have a solitary chop left from yesterday's barbecue. I have eaten this made with both pork and goat, but lamb or beef would be good, too.

SERVES 4

4tbsp. sour cream	4–6oz. barbecued meat, cut up or shredded, heated through
grated rind of ¼ lime	1 avocado, peeled, pitted, and sliced
juice of ½ lime	3–5 radishes, diced
1 chorizo or spicy blood sausage, such as morcilla	handful of watercress leaves, coarsely chopped
4 chalupa shapes or 8 Garnachas (page 42)	fresh salsa of choice
1 recipe Refried Black Beans (page 76), warmed	
about ¾ cup crumbled white crumbly cheese, such as not too salty feta or fresh pecorino	

1. Combine the sour cream with the lime rind and juice. Set aside.

2. Pan brown the sausage until crisp and browned; set aside and keep warm.

3. Preheat the oven to 400°. Heat the chalupa shapes on a baking sheet in the oven for about 15–20 minutes or until warm.

4. Fill each chalupa with warm beans, then sprinkle with cheese. Top with a little of the browned sausage, the barbecued meat, diced avocado, radishes, watercress, and a spoonful of the lime-flavored cream. Offer salsa of choice on the side.

NUTRITIONAL INFORMATION				
	TOTAL FAT	SAT FAT	CHOL	ENERGY
Total	234g	66g	245mg	4468kcals
Per Serving	58g	17g	61mg	1117kcals

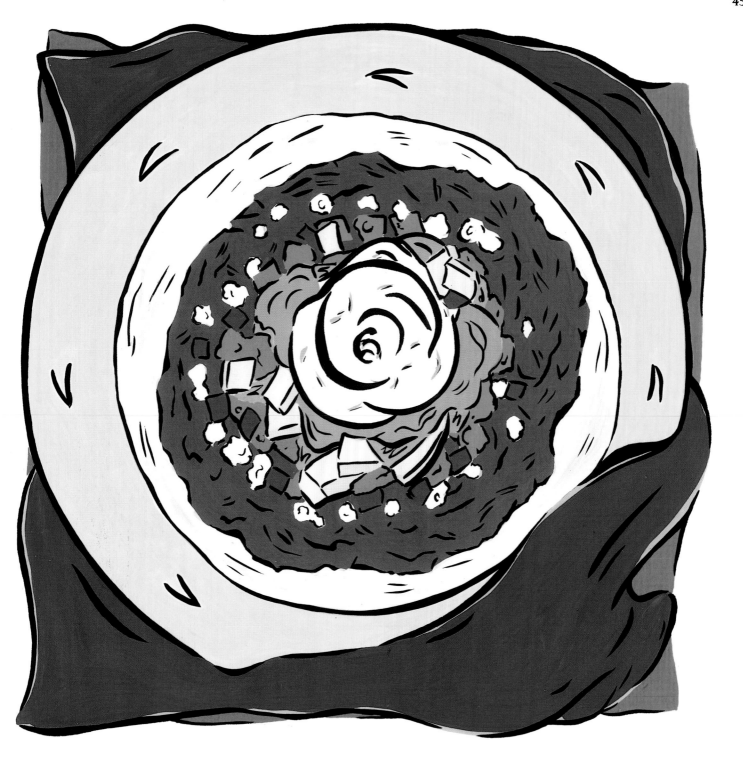

NARANJA CON CHILE A LA YUCATECA
YUCATECAN ORANGES

Outside the ruins of Chichen Itza, on a day thick with jungle heat, I cooled myself with the following snack purchased from a makeshift stall. It is a classic nibble in the Yucatán, where the juicy citrus flavor combined with the hot pepper is cooling; the small amount of salt is surprisingly refreshing since it helps retain liquid that is so easily evaporating in the relentless heat.

SERVES 4

4 ripe oranges, peeled, seeded and sliced

cayenne pepper to taste

paprika to taste

sugar and salt as liked

1. Arrange the oranges on a plate, including their juices.

2. Sprinkle with cayenne, paprika, sugar, and salt.

3. Let chill for 1 hour or so before serving.

NUTRITIONAL INFORMATION

	TOTAL FAT	SAT FAT	CHOL	ENERGY
Total	0g	0g	0mg	237kcals
Per Serving	0g	0g	0mg	59kcals

VARIATION
OTHER FRUITS

Ripe sweet mangos sliced and splashed with lime juice, or pineapple chunks, sliced melon or watermelon are all delicious prepared as for the above oranges.

TAMALES DE ELOTE
FRESH CORN TAMALES

Tamales are often sold from tamale vendors, fished out from big pots that are fragrant with the smell of steaming corn husks. Tamales may be filled with savory ingredients or with sweet ones. During the season of the sweetest corn, they are made with fresh corn such as these.

SERVES 4

corn husks	½ cup water or as needed
6tbsp. butter, softened	2 onions, toasted and diced
8oz. masa	salt and black pepper or mild chili powder to taste
½tsp. baking powder	
2¼ cups cooked corn kernels (canned is fine; use the liquid when required)	dash sugar, if needed
	salsa of choice, preferably tangy lemon-limy salsa

1. Place the corn husks in a bowl and pour boiling water over them to cover. Cover the bowl and let soften for about 30 minutes.

2. Using a wooden spoon or food processor, combine the butter with the masa and baking powder.

3. Blend the corn in a blender or food processor until it forms a chunky purée, with half of the corn still in kernels, the rest a creamy mixture.

4. Work the corn purée into the masa-butter mixture, then continue adding water until it forms the consistency desired – moist but not too sticky, firm but not hard and crumbly.

5. Place two or three corn husks on a plate or in the palm of your hand. On top of this, place several spoonfuls of the filling, onions and season to taste. Fold over, first the sides, then the top and bottom, to fully enclose the filling.

6. Place each husk-wrapped package in the top of a steamer, then steam the packages for 40 minutes or until they feel firm. After 30 minutes take one out to sample it. Top up the water as needed.

7. Serve the tamales either right away, or reheat later or the next day. Accompany with salsa of choice.

NUTRITIONAL INFORMATION				
	TOTAL FAT	SAT FAT	CHOL	ENERGY
Total	69g	42g	173mg	1790kcals
Per Serving	17g	10g	43mg	448kcals

VARIATION
CHILI CHEESE TAMALES

Fresh corn tamales are delicious with the addition of roasted mild green chili and white cheese. Choose a roasted, peeled, seeded, and sliced poblano or Anaheim chili. Select a cheese such as Cheddar or combination of Cheddar and tangy mild white goat's cheese. Place a nugget of each inside the corn filling, then fold and wrap as above.

APPERATIVE DE JICAMA

JICAMA SNACK OR APPETIZER
WITH CHILI

On a hot, sultry day there are few foods lighter and more refreshing than sliced jicama, sprinkled with salt, fiery cayenne chili, and a splash of lime juice. Jicama is a root whose white flesh looks very much like a potato and tastes somewhat like an apple.

Sold in the streets of many Mexican towns, they are often skewered with fruit, to be nibbled while you continue along your way, but they are equally good arranged on a platter and eaten sitting down.

Watermelon, pineapple, mango (either ripe or green), papaya, and oranges are all delicious added to the fruit plate (I omit the salt when including the other, sweeter, fruits).

SERVES 4

½ medium jicama, peeled and cut into bite-sized pieces	cayenne pepper to taste
½ lime	salt to taste

1. Arrange the jicama on a plate and squeeze the lime over. Chill if liked.

2. When ready to serve, sprinkle with cayenne and salt to taste.

VARIATION
GREEN MANGO

Peel 1–2 green mangos and remove the pit. Cut into small bite-sized slices. Sprinkle with lime, cayenne, and salt to taste. Let stand for at least 30 minutes, then eat as liked.

GARBANZOS CON CHILES

GARBANZO BEANS WITH SALSA, CILANTRO, AND LIME

On every street and village throughout Mexico at various times of the day, vendors set up simple stalls and sell a variety of foods. In Guadalajara I often bought the following snack of tender boiled garbanzo beans, wrapped in a paper cone, splashed with salsa and lime. Spicy and hot they are irresistible for afternoon walking and munching. Amounts don't matter much – your own personal taste is all. Use the following as a guide only.

SERVES 4

1lb. cooked drained garbanzo beans (canned are fine)	3–5tbsp. chopped fresh cilantro
salt to taste	1 onion, finely chopped
hot salsa or bottled hot sauce as liked	wedges of lime

1. Season the garbanzo beans with salt to taste. Mix with the salsa or hot sauce, cilantro, and onion. Serve at room temperature, with wedges of lime to squeeze over.

NUTRITIONAL INFORMATION

	TOTAL FAT	SAT FAT	CHOL	ENERGY
Total	13g	1g	0mg	545kcals
Per Serving	3g	0.3g	0mg	136kcals

BEBIDAS

COOLING DRINKS

On any sweltering day, by the time the sun has barely made its way up, stalls are already set up for refreshing fruit drinks. Blenders whirling away turn out creamy refreshments of milk, fruit, juices, and drinks based on crushed ice.

LIQUADA DES FRUTAS

FRUIT MILKSHAKES

FROM THE STREETS OF MEXICO

In every street, marketplace, and bus station you will find counters piled high with fragrant sweet fruit. Again blenders whirling away, stopping every so often to pour out big glasses of sweet fruit drinks. Sometimes a little yogurt is added; at other times no milk at all, simply tropical fruits and their juices. Though strawberries sound rather pedestrian, they are worth noting for their exquisite refreshment, and because I will never forget the sweet pink glassfuls that got me through my first hot and sweaty visit to Mexico's capital city.

SERVES 2

8oz. strawberries	few drops vanilla extract
2tbsp. confectioners' sugar	crushed ice
1 cup milk	

1. Whirl all the ingredients together in a blender until frothy. Drink right away.

NUTRITIONAL INFORMATION				
	TOTAL FAT	SAT FAT	CHOL	ENERGY
Total	0.5g	0.25g	2mg	229kcals
Per Serving	0.25g	0.1g	1mg	114kcals

VARIATIONS

Other fruits to choose when making milkshakes: cantaloupe, apricots, bananas, peach. Try mango using yogurt instead of milk. And do try papaya, pineapple and/or watermelon using water or white grape juice instead of milk.

HORCHATA CON FRUTAS

SWEET RICE-MILK

WITH TROPICAL FRUIT AND NUTS

Horchata is made by soaking uncooked rice in flavored water until it softens, then puréeing it with sugar and flavorings. It makes a nourishing, comforting, and refreshing drink with a "milky" consistency but completely non-dairy.

SERVES 4

generous 1 cup rice

4¼ cups water

1 4-inch cinnamon stick, broken into several pieces

3tbsp. pecans

¼–½tsp. vanilla extract

⅓ cup sugar or to taste

2 cactus fruits, peeled and sieved to deseed (or mango, peeled, pitted, and diced)

½–1 sweet ripe melon, such as cantaloupe or Galia, peeled, seeded, and diced

juice of ½ lime

1. Combine the rice, water, and cinnamon stick and leave overnight at room temperature or in the refrigerator.

2. When the rice is softened the next day, remove the cinnamon stick.

3. Place the rice in the blender with the pecans, vanilla extract, and sugar. Purée until quite smooth.

4. Add the cactus fruit, melon, and lime juice, and repeat whirling in the blender.

5. Serve right away, strained through a sieve, and poured over ice cubes. Since the rice settles and the drink separates quite quickly, horchata should be freshly blended just before serving. (May be prepared ahead of time, up until the adding of the fruit. Blend with the fruit just before serving.)

NUTRITIONAL INFORMATION				
	TOTAL FAT	SAT FAT	CHOL	ENERGY
Total	34g	2.5g	0mg	1521kcals
Per Serving	8.5g	0.5g	0mg	380kcals

VARIATION
TIME SAVING

Use rice powder instead of steeping whole rice overnight. Combine rice powder with milk, sugar or honey to taste, vanilla, and cinnamon. Blend with crushed ice until frothy, then serve immediately.

MARISCOS

THE SEAFOOD STALL

From seaside villages to cities such as the capital Mexico City, tiny shacks and restaurants dot the streets serving fresh, briny seafood.

COCKTEL DE MARISCOS

SEAFOOD COCKTAIL
WITH CHILIS, ORANGE, AND GREEN ONION

Any seafood could be used here: plump shrimp, rings of chewy squid, mussels plucked from their shells.
The fiery citrus salsa is typical of salsas from the Southeastern coast of Mexico, from Vera Cruz south through the Yucatan. A drop or two is probably all you will need; save leftovers for brightening up nearly anything else – soups and stews, tacos, seafood, broiled foods, rice, and beans. If your chilis are not blisteringly hot, you might want to increase the amount so that the sauce packs a good punch; if your chilis are terribly hot, decrease amounts to about half that called for (it should be spicy, not painful).

SERVES 4

4–6 green onions, thinly sliced

½ red habanero chili, roasted, charred, peeled, seeded, and coarsely chopped

½–1 fresh red chili, such as jalapeño, roasted, charred, peeled, seeded, and coarsely chopped

½ cup orange juice, plus a little pulp

⅓ cup lime juice, preferably freshly squeezed

salt to taste

1lb. shrimp in their shells

round or Romaine lettuce leaves

1 lime, cut into wedges

1 orange, cut into wedges

1. Combine the green onions with habanero and jalapeño chilis, then stir in the orange juice, lime juice, and salt. Let stand for at least 10 minutes, preferably up to 3 hours.
2. Cook the shrimp over high heat until bubbles form around the edge, remove from the heat, and let cool. Then drain, peel and slit down the backs, removing the veins. Serve the cooked seafood on leaves of crisp lettuce and sprinkle a few drops of the sauce onto them. Serve with lime and orange wedges and additional hot sauce.

NUTRITIONAL INFORMATION				
	TOTAL FAT	SAT FAT	CHOL	ENERGY
Total	4g	1g	473mg	333kcals
Per Serving	1g	0.25g	118mg	83kcals

VARIATION
Instead of shrimp, try 1lb. squid, cleaned and cut into rings and tentacles, 2lb. clams or mussels, or any other fresh seafood or combination that is available.

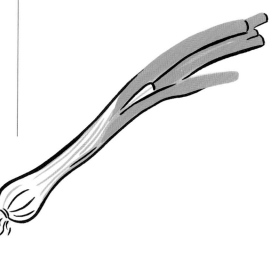

CEVICHE

MARINATED AND CITRUS-PICKLED FISH APPETIZER

SERVES 4

1lb. fish fillets (haddock, sole, snapper, sierra or similar), skinned and bones removed

¾ cup freshly squeezed lemon juice (juice of 3 lemons)

¾ cup freshly squeezed lime juice (juice of 3 limes)

2tsp. oregano leaves, crushed

½tsp. cumin seeds, lightly toasted and left whole

2 ripe tomatoes, finely diced

1 small to medium red onion, chopped

1–2 green serrano chilis, chopped or as liked

4tbsp. chopped fresh cilantro

2tbsp. chopped fresh mint

1 stalk celery, chopped or thinly sliced

10–15 pimento-stuffed green olives, sliced

2tbsp. sliced jalapeños en escabeche (pickled jalapeño chilis) or as liked

½ cup freshly squeezed orange juice

1tsp. salt or to taste

2tbsp. olive oil

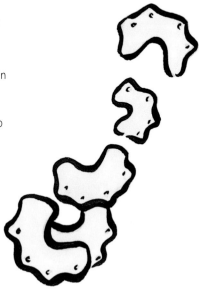

1. Cut the fish into ½ inch cubes. Place in a glass container with the lemon juice, lime juice, and oregano. Mix well, then cover and leave in the refrigerator overnight. Do not leave for longer than 12 hours or the fish will go mushy.

2. Drain the fish and add the toasted cumin seeds, tomatoes, onion, chili, cilantro, mint, celery, green olives, jalapeños en escabeche, orange juice, salt, and olive oil.

3. Chill before serving. This dish can be refrigerated for up to 3 days.

NUTRITIONAL INFORMATION				
	TOTAL FAT	SAT FAT	CHOL	ENERGY
Total	29g	4g	162mg	714kcals
Per Serving	7g	1g	41mg	178kcals

FIAMBRE DE JAIBA

SPICY CRAB SALAD

In the Yucatan, where temperatures soar to almost unbearable heights, you will find salady dishes called fiambre – cool mixtures of hot and spicy ingredients. Their flash of hot chili and cool crisp texture refresh and stimulate appetites grown sluggish from the assault of the day's heat. Often these fiambres are rolled up in tender fresh tortillas for hot-weather tacos.

SERVES 4

3 shallots or ¼ red onion, finely chopped

1 fresh chili, such as jalapeño or serrano, chopped

juice of ½ lime

1 tbsp. white wine or fruit vinegar

1 tsp. fresh marjoram or ½ tsp. chopped fresh oregano

1 tsp. chopped fresh cilantro

1 tbsp. olive oil

8–12 oz. fresh crab meat

1 avocado, peeled and sliced

radishes, thinly sliced

1. Combine the shallots or onion with the chili, lime juice, vinegar, marjoram, cilantro, and olive oil. Mix lightly with the crab.

2. Serve garnished with the avocado and radishes.

NUTRITIONAL INFORMATION				
	TOTAL FAT	SAT FAT	CHOL	ENERGY
Total	52g	9g	162mg	682kcals
Per Serving	13g	2g	41mg	170kcals

VARIATION

Chilis Rellenos con Fiambre: Omit the chili from the filling mixture. Prepare large green chilis, such as poblano or Anaheim, by roasting, peeling and removing the inner core and seeds. Fill with the above crab mixture and serve chilled, on a bed of lettuce, garnished with avocado and radishes.

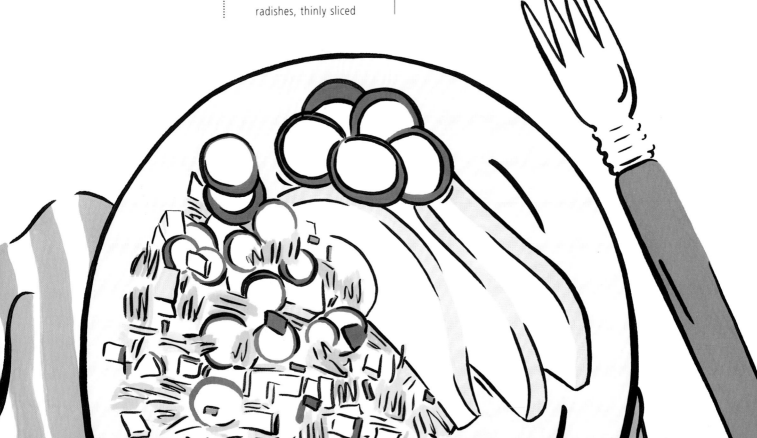

CHAPTER THREE

THE HOME KITCHEN

THE HOME KITCHEN

DIPS, NACHOS, MELTED CHEESE DISHES, CUP TAMALES, SOUPS

The best Mexican food is rarely found in restaurants, even in Mexico. It is a unique blend of Central American, of Spanish, and of the Arab cooking which in its turn influenced Spain. It can be brutally simple, or extremely complex: indeed, the same dish may well be prepared in ways which reflect the various influences in very varying degrees, so you may have an Aztec version, a poor Spanish soldiers' version, a rich hidalgo's version, and a Moorish version. Here are several recipes that are found throughout Mexico, in almost every home – everyday, staple, simple dishes.

TOTOPOS O NACHOS CON ELOTES Y FRIJOLES

BLACK BEAN AND CORN NACHOS

Nachos are simply toasted tortilla chips, topped with cheese and salsa and melted in the oven. From this basic beginning, nachos have come to encompass many delicious appetizers based on crisp tortilla chips.

SERVES 4 – 6

1 onion, chopped

3 cloves garlic, chopped

2tbsp. olive oil

2tsp. mild chili powder, such as ancho, or pasilla or mixture that includes chipotle powder

1–1½lb. cooked black beans, plus about ½ cup of their cooking liquid

salt and hot sauce to taste

1tsp. cumin seeds

10oz. Cheddar cheese, thinly sliced

about 1½ cups corn kernels, drained and warmed

3tbsp. chopped fresh cilantro

10 tiny tomatoes, quartered, or 2 ripe medium tomatoes, diced

1–2tbsp. pickled jalapeños

tortilla chips, preferably low salt

1. Preheat the oven to 450°. Sauté the onion and garlic in the olive oil until softened, then sprinkle with chili powder and cook a moment or two longer.

2. Add the black beans and their liquid, then cook down until it forms a thick paste. Mash the beans slightly as they cook. Season with salt and hot sauce to taste.

3. Spoon the bean mixture into a baking dish, then sprinkle with cumin seeds and cheese.

4. Bake until the cheese melts, then remove from the oven and spoon the warm corn around the edges. Sprinkle with the cilantro and garnish with the tomatoes and pickled jalapeños. Serve right away, accompanied by tortilla chips arranged around the edge in a sunflower-like pattern.

NUTRITIONAL INFORMATION				
	TOTAL FAT	SAT FAT	CHOL	ENERGY
Total	146g	68g	275mg	2644kcalsJ
Per Serving (4)	36g	17g	69mg	661kcals
Per Serving (6)	24g	11g	46mg	441kcalsJ

GUACAMOLE

The word Guacamole comes from the Nahuatl molli, meaning sauce, and aguacate, meaning avocado. This classic sauce can be varied at will: more onion or less, salsa for seasoning instead of the individual ingredients, a few pureed tomatillos instead of tomatoes.

Spoon it into chicken soup for sopa de aguacate; roll into warm corn tortillas for a quintessential family snack or picnic treat; spread over crisp tortillas it makes a sauce for tostadas compuestas.

Guacamole is eaten as a sauce for carne asado, spit-roasted chicken or even hamburgers (hamburguesas); and is there a more enticing snack than a bowl of freshly made guacamole surrounded by crisp tortilla chips?

Choosing the avocados is the most important part of the recipe. They should be black or dark-skinned, and firm to the touch with a slight give at the pointed top that indicates a softening flesh. If they are too soft and squishy, they may taste off. Even if you have somewhat past-it avocados, you can usually pare off the browned bits once the fruit is peeled. When avocados are too hard at the time of purchase they may never ripen, so they should always be at least slightly yielding when purchased.

To open, cut into halves and remove the pit. Scoop out the flesh with a spoon.

SERVES 4–6

3 ripe black avocados	salt and mild chili pepper to taste
juice of 1–1½ lemons or limes	cayenne or Tabasco if needed
1 clove garlic, chopped	about ¼ hot green chili, chopped
½ small to medium onion, chopped	¼tsp. ground cumin (optional)
2–3 small to medium tomatoes, diced or chopped	1tbsp. chopped fresh cilantro

1. Coarsely mash the avocado with the lemon or lime juices. Mix with the garlic, onion, tomatoes, salt, mild chili, cayenne or Tabasco if using, green chili, cumin, and cilantro.

2. Mix lightly but well and season to taste.

NUTRITIONAL INFORMATION				
	TOTAL FAT	SAT FAT	CHOL	ENERGY
Total	96g	23g	0mg	971kcals
Per Serving (4)	24g	6g	0mg	243kcals
Per Serving (6)	16g	4g	0mg	162kcals

QUESO OAXAQUENO AL FORNO

BAKED WHITE CHEESE
WITH GREEN SALSA

In Oaxaca this dish would be prepared with queso Oaxaca, a milky fresh cheese somewhere between fresh mozzarella and fresh pecorino. Don't let the simplicity of the recipe fool you into thinking it is regular,: the taste of fresh milky cheese with sharp green salsa, all warmed together, is memorable.

SERVES 4

2 balls of fresh mozzarella or other milky, slightly but not too salty, fresh cheese, sliced	about 1 cup Salsa Verde (page 68), or to taste
1 cup cooked tomatillos, puréed or chopped	8 corn tortillas, warmed

1. Preheat the oven to 400°. Arrange the cheese in a large baking dish or in individual ramekins.

2. Combine the tomatillos and salsa verde, then pour over cheese.

3. Bake for about 10 minutes or until the cheese melts softly and bubbles around the edges.

4. Serve right away, accompanied by warm corn tortillas for dipping or for making tacos.

NUTRITIONAL INFORMATION				
	TOTAL FAT	SAT FAT	CHOL	ENERGY
Total	40g	22g	111mg	1575kcals
Per Serving	10g	5.5g	28mg	394kcals

SNACK SOUPS

Though you are apt to find them in cafés and sold from street vendors, soup is a
fixture of the Mexican home kitchen. No stove, it seems, is without a simmering
pot full at any given time. Soups make comforting midnight snacks after a night
of too much tequila, or a nourishing bowlful on a cool evening to follow a
sultry day.

CALDO RANCHERA

RICH SPICY BROTH

WITH PUMPKIN OR PARSNIP, GARBANZO BEANS, MACARONI, CABBAGE, AND CHEESE

This is a homely soup I have had spooned up in a little café
one mild evening somewhere in the labyrinth-like streets of
Mexico City.

SERVES 4 – 6

4¼ cups chicken or other
flavorful stock

1 cup water

about 1½ cups parsnip or
pumpkin, cut into bite-sized
pieces (peeled if pumpkin)

1 onion, chopped

3 cloves garlic, chopped

2 tomatoes, diced

2 bay leaves

4tbsp. chopped fresh
cilantro

8oz. macaroni, cooked and
drained

1⅓ cups cooked drained
garbanzo beans

½ fresh red chili, such as
jalapeño, thinly sliced

¼ cabbage, thinly sliced

1–1½ cups shredded mild
white cheese

½ pickled jalapeño chili,
chopped, or to taste (or a
little chipotle)

1 lime, cut into wedges

1. Combine the stock with the water, parsnip or pumpkin,
onion, garlic, tomatoes, bay leaves, and half the cilantro. Bring
to a boil then reduce the heat and simmer until the vegetables
are quite tender. Taste for seasoning.

2. Add the macaroni, garbanzo beans, fresh red chili, and
cabbage, and cook only a moment or two, to warm through.

3. Ladle into bowls and garnish each with a little jalapeño , a
sprinkle of the remaining cilantro, and a wedge of lime.

NUTRITIONAL INFORMATION				
	TOTAL FAT	SAT FAT	CHOL	ENERGY
Total	45g	23g	100mg	1101kcals
Per Serving (4)	11g	6g	25mg	275kcals
Per Serving (6)	7.5g	4g	17mg	183kcals

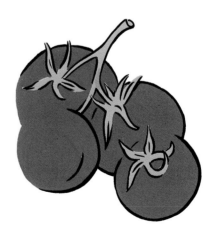

CALDO TLAPENO
CHICKEN SOUP
WITH AVOCADO, GARBANZO BEANS, AND CHIPOTLES

Caldo Tlapeno – that bowl of rich clear chicken soup awash with small pieces of chicken and vegetables, studded with garbanzo beans and spiked with smoky hot chipotle chilis, has gone from being ladled out by street vendors to becoming a classic in the Mexican kitchen.

The soup is said to have originated in the Mexico City suburb of Tlapan, where on Sundays, the park came alive with families spending the day in the open air amid the greenery. The food vendors, each trying to capture the appetite of the strolling diners, concocted and added various ingredients to their dishes, in the hopes of selling their wares. One soup-seller hit upon the simple combination we think of today as Tlapan: avocado, chipotle, garbanzo beans, chicken stock, and lime.

SERVES 4 – 6

3 cloves garlic, coarsely chopped

1tbsp. olive oil

2 zucchini, cut into bite-sized pieces

½ carrot, thinly sliced

4¼ cups chicken stock

2 cups cooked drained garbanzo beans

1–2 chipotle chilis en adobo, cut into strips, plus a little of the marinade

2 green onions, thinly sliced

about 1 cup shredded chicken

1 avocado, peeled, pitted, and diced

1tbsp. chopped fresh cilantro

handful of tortilla chips, preferably low salt ones

1 lime, cut into wedges

1. Warm the garlic in the olive oil without browning. Add the zucchini, carrot, chicken stock, and garbanzo beans, then bring to a boil. Reduce the heat and simmer for about 10 minutes or until vegetables are tender.

2. Ladle the soup into bowls and garnish each with a little chipotle, green onions, shredded chicken, avocado, cilantro, tortilla chips, and wedges of lime.

NUTRITIONAL INFORMATION				
	TOTAL FAT	SAT FAT	CHOL	ENERGY
Total	78g	14g	76mg	1450kcals
Per Serving (4)	20g	3.5g	19mg	363kcals
Per Serving (6)	13g	2.5g	13mg	242kcals

VARIATION
POSOLE TLAPENO

Simmer cooked drained hominy in place of the garbanzo beans and garnish as before. The earthy, bland hominy is sensational with the smoky hot chipotle, creamy avocado, and sharp tangy lime.

GAZPACHO CON NOPALES

SPICY GAZPACHO

WITH CACTUS

Gazpacho is thirst-quenching and cooling in any hot, parched climate. It becomes exotic and spicy in Mexico where the sharpness of lime, the dusting of earthy cumin, tropical vegetables such as tomatillos and cactus, pungent herbs such as cilantro, flavor this invigorating bowlful. For extra crunch, use jicama in place of cucumber.

I like to keep a large pitcher full in my refrigerator – it can get one through the cruellest of heatwaves. On particularly languid nights, a drop of tequila or even vodka added enhances its refreshment.

SERVES 4 – 6

3 cloves garlic, chopped

2 cups tomato juice

2 cups stock, such as vegetable or beef

2 medium or 1 large cucumber, diced

1–2 ripe tomatoes, diced

1 cup cooked tomatillos, skins removed and lightly cut up or crushed

1 cactus pod, cooked and drained and cut into bite-sized pieces (or use canned, drained)

¼ cup olive oil

2tbsp. red or white wine vinegar or lime juice

1tbsp. cumin

salt, pepper, thyme and hot sauce to taste

about 8 small ice cubes

1. Combine all the ingredients and stir together to combine well. Chill for at least 2 hours.

2. Adjust the seasoning of salt, hot pepper, and vinegar; cold foods usually need quite a bit of salt and hot pepper.

3. Serve each portion of gazpacho with 1 or 2 small ice cubes.

NUTRITIONAL INFORMATION			
	TOTAL FAT	SAT FAT	CHOL	ENERGY
Total	51g	7g	0mg	639kcals
Per Serving (4)	13g	2g	0mg	160kcals
Per Serving (6)	9g	1g	0mg	107kcals

HUEVOS RANCHEROS

EGGS ON TORTILLAS

TOMATO-PEPPER SAUCE

Huevos rancheros is ubiquitous in Mexico; it can be served as a midnight feast or a late morning meal to start the day, or whenever. The dish is often served differently but it is always the same: tender eggs on a tortilla, blanketed in tomato-chili sauce. Garnishes may vary: browned chorizo, broiled plantains or bananas, a covering of melted cheese, slices of avocado, a puddle of warm refried beans, a flurry of sliced fiery chilis on top of the salsa, a sprinkling of cilantro. Sautéed mild green poblano chilis (rajas) make an excellent accompaniment. No matter how varied the dish might be, it always tastes utterly delicious: the eggs free-range and fresh, the sauce alive with fire and flavor.

SERVES 4

4 tortillas, warmed (page 74)

8 poached or gently fried eggs with runny yolks

2 cups warmed Cooked Tomato Sauce, (page 77)

1 tbsp. chopped fresh cilantro

1 or 2 fresh green chilis, such as jalapeño or serrano, thinly sliced

1. Place a tortilla on each plate.

2. Top each tortilla with 2 cooked eggs.

3. Spoon over the warm tomato-chili sauce, then sprinkle with cilantro and chili. Serve right away.

NUTRITIONAL INFORMATION				
	TOTAL FAT	SAT FAT	CHOL	ENERGY
Total	70g	20g	1585mg	1513kcals
Per Serving	17.5g	5g	396mg	378kcals

VARIATIONS

HUEVOS MICHOACAN

Garnish with a little chopped chipotles, their adobo marinade or salsa, and diced browned bananas or plantains.

HUEVOS DEL CAMPESINA

Serve the egg-topped tortillas with a chunky rather than puréed sauce: sauté 2 onions with garlic and diced green pepper, then sprinkle with 1tsp. ground cumin and ¼tsp. cinnamon. Cook for a moment or two, then add 2lb. diced tomatoes (either raw or first toasted and charred, then peeled before dicing). Simmer until saucelike and chunky. Season with salt and sugar to balance the acid-sweetness, then serve over the eggs. Garnish with chopped fresh cilantro.

SOPA DE LIMA

YUCATECAN LIME SOUP
WITH TOASTED GARLIC AND CITRUS JUICES

Traditionally, this tangy soup is served with shredded chicken and chicken giblets added to the bowl. I like the lighter version below, with the meat and giblets saved for another dish: tacos, tortas, or enchiladas.

SERVES 4 – 6

3 medium onions, finely chopped

2–3 limes, peeled, seeded, and diced

2–3 serrano chilis, finely chopped

½ green pepper, chopped

1–1½ tbsp. olive oil

3–4 ripe tomatoes, diced (fresh is best)

dash oregano, crushed

salt and pepper

10–15 cloves whole garlic, toasted in their skins, then peeled

4¼ cups chicken stock

juice of ½ grapefruit, plus a little grated rind

juice of ½ orange, plus a little grated rind

2 tbsp. finely chopped fresh cilantro

handful of tortilla chips, preferably low salt ones

1. Combine 1 chopped onion with the diced lime flesh and chopped chilis. Set aside.

2. Sauté the remaining onions with the green pepper in the olive oil until softened. Add the tomatoes, oregano, salt and pepper, toasted peeled garlic, and chicken stock.

3. Bring to a boil, then reduce the heat and simmer for about 10 minutes or until the tomatoes are just cooked through and the soup is richly flavored.

4. Just before serving, add the grapefruit and orange juice and rind, and the cilantro.

5. Place several tablespoons of the onion-chili-lime mixture into each bowl, then ladle in the hot soup. Serve each bowlful garnished with tortilla chips.

NUTRITIONAL INFORMATION				
	TOTAL FAT	SAT FAT	CHOL	ENERGY
Total	36g	6g	0mg	806kcals
Per Serving (4)	9g	1.5g	0mg	202kcals
Per Serving (6)	6g	1g	0mg	134kcals

CHAPTER FOUR

THE SALSA BAR

★ ★ ★ ★ ★

THE SALSA BAR

Salsa literally means "sauce," but in the absence of other qualifications it normally means salsa cruda, "raw sauce," which appears on the table as regularly as pepper and salt. It is frequently used as a dip, with corn chips, but it can be spooned on to almost any savory dish: omelets, chiles rellenos, meat . . . you name it. There are also cooked salsas and, whether raw or cooked, most salsas improve and mature (grow hotter!) if left overnight in the refrigerator. The basic ingredients, mixed-and-matched in a wide variety of combinations, are dried or fresh peppers; onions; tomatoes (including tomatillos); garlic, and cilantro. Optional additions include oregano, vinegar, and olive oil.

SALSA CRUDA

BASIC MEXICAN SALSA OF UNCOOKED INGREDIENTS

This raw salsa is classic: for best flavor and fragrance, as well as maximum heat, make it freshly before serving. You can use fresh unpeeled tomatoes during high season; in the middle of winter, use canned. As for peeling – it is up to you.

2–3 cloves garlic, chopped

1 small to medium onion, chopped

1–2 fresh green chilis, such as jalapeño or serrano, or as desired, chopped

5–8 ripe tomatoes, diced or chopped

3tbsp. chopped fresh cilantro

salt to taste, sugar if needed to balance the acid of the tomatoes

cumin to taste (optional)

1. Combine all the salsa ingredients together.

NUTRITIONAL INFORMATION				
	TOTAL FAT	SAT FAT	CHOL	ENERGY
Total	1.75g	0.5g	0mg	116kcals

SALSA DE FRUTAS

TROPICAL FRUIT SALSA

A selection of tropical fruit, diced and tossed with a little chili and a squeeze of lime juice, makes a refreshing salsa that is especially good with broiled seafood or meat tacos.

¼ ripe sweet pineapple, peeled and diced

½ mango or papaya, peeled, seeded and diced

1 slice crisp watermelon, seeded and diced, or ¼ apple, seeded and diced, or 1 banana, peeled and diced

½–1 green chili, such as jalapeño or serrano, chopped

½–1 red chili, such as jalapeño or serrano, chopped

¼ red onion, chopped

1tbsp. sugar

salt to taste

juice of ¼ lime

1. Combine all the salsa ingredients together and taste for seasoning. Serve right away.

NUTRITIONAL INFORMATION				
	TOTAL FAT	SAT FAT	CHOL	ENERGY
Total	0.75g	0.1g	0mg	189kcals

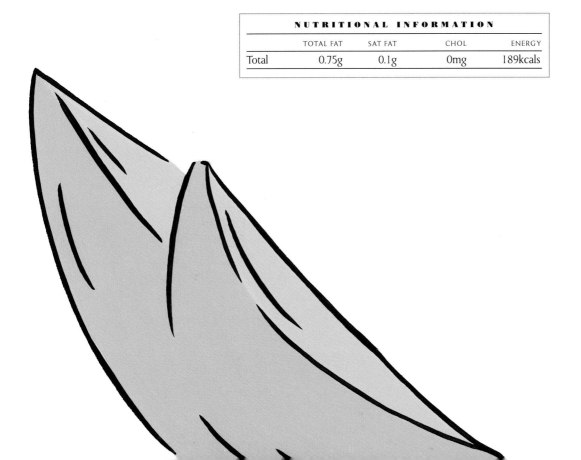

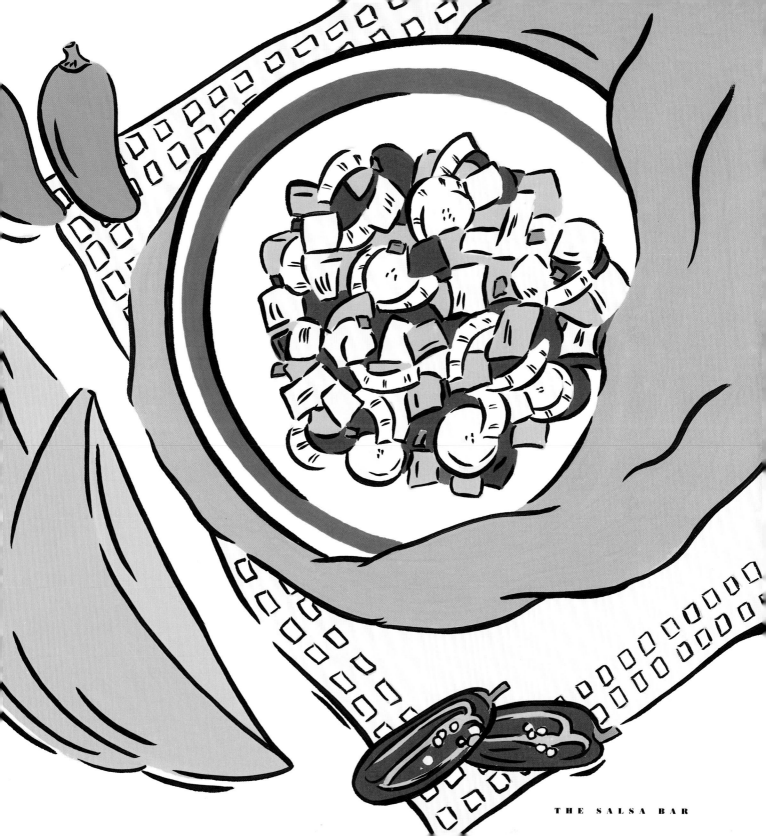

SALSA COCIDO DE JITOMATE Y CHILE FRESCO

COOKED TOMATO AND FRESH CHILI SALSA

2–3 fresh green chilis, such as guero or Anaheim or poblano

6–8 medium tomatoes (use fresh, not canned for this recipe)

2–3 cloves garlic, chopped

salt to taste

juice of ½ lemon or lime

oregano to taste

1. Place the chilis in a saucepan with water to cover. Boil covered, for 5–10 minutes or until the chilis are tender. Remove from the liquid and leave until cool enough to handle.

2. While the chilis are cooling, place the tomatoes in saucepan with water to just cover and bring to a boil. Cook over a high heat for about 5–8 minutes or until the tomatoes are tender and liquid partly evaporated. Remove the tomato skins out of the mixture and discard.

3. Cut the stems off the chilis and remove the skin and seeds. Coarsely chop the flesh.

4. Using a mortar and pestle or blender, purée the garlic with salt. Work in the chili flesh, then the tomato flesh, adding just enough of the tomato cooking liquid to form a smoothish sauce.

5. Season with lemon juice and oregano to taste, and more salt if needed.

NUTRITIONAL INFORMATION			
	TOTAL FAT	SAT FAT	CHOL	ENERGY
Total	2g	0.5g	0mg	112kcals

SALSA VERDE DE TOMATILLO

GREEN SALSA OF CHILIS AND TOMATILLOS

Husk tomatoes, astringent and sour, are at their best cooked into a tart purée and used as a basis for the green sauces, or salsas, that form refreshing contrast to the richer dishes. This makes a delicious salsa of cooked tomatillas combined with raw onion, garlic, and cilantro; for a sauce to use for cooking, the aromatics will be stewed with the tomatillas. This salsa has just a little bite – for a more aggressive character add more (or hotter) chilis. For a milder sauce, use only one chili combined with one chopped green bell pepper. Use the mild sauce to cook with: simmer with chicken or pork for classic green chili dishes.

1lb. tomatillos, quartered, or 1lb. can tomatillos

1–2 fresh hot chilis, such as jalapeños, chopped

1 small onion, chopped

2 cloves garlic, chopped

1tbsp. chopped fresh cilantro

salt and cumin to taste

1. If using raw tomatillos, quarter and place them in a saucepan with water to cover. Bring to a boil, then reduce the heat and simmer until soft but not too mushy, about 10 minutes. Drain gently, saving some of the liquid in case you need it for the salsa. If using canned tomatillos, do not cook, just open the can and gently drain.

2. Place the cooked or canned tomatillos in a blender or processor with the chilis, onion, garlic, and cilantro. Blend until the mixture reaches the consistency desired: it may be preferred smoother or chunkier. Add a little of the cooking liquid if needed, for consistency.

3. Season to taste with salt and cumin.

NUTRITIONAL INFORMATION			
	TOTAL FAT	SAT FAT	CHOL	ENERGY
Total	0.5g	neg	0mg	102kcals

"DOG SNOUT" SALSA

This Yucatecan salsa is fiery hot. It is said to be called Dog Snout because its pungent fumes make one's nose run uncontrollably, like the wet nose of a dog!

2 habanero or Scots bonnet chilis, or more if preferred

2 cloves garlic, toasted

1tsp. salt

juice of ½ orange, plus grated rind of ¼ orange

juice of ½ lime

⅛tsp. oregano, crushed

2–3 green onions, thinly sliced

1tbsp. chopped fresh cilantro

1. Purée the chilis with the garlic, salt, orange juice, orange rind, and lime juice.

2. Season with oregano, then stir in the green onions and cilantro.

NUTRITIONAL INFORMATION			
	TOTAL FAT	SAT FAT	CHOL	ENERGY
Total	0.2g	neg	0mg	22kcals

HOT DRIED RED CHILI SAUCE

Make a double or triple quantity of this powerful sauce; it keeps at least a month and is handy to shake onto anything that needs a bit of fire.

5 or smallish dried hot red chilis (such as cayenne or Arbol; don't use bird's eye as they are too hot)

½ cup white wine vinegar

½tsp. salt

1. Crumble the chilis into small pieces. Purée the chilis with the vinegar and salt.

NUTRITIONAL INFORMATION			
	TOTAL FAT	SAT FAT	CHOL	ENERGY
Total	0g	0g	0mg	29kcals

SCORCHED CHILI SALSA

Lightly scorching the chilis imparts a slightly smoky taste, and makes the little peppers easy to peel. *Take care of your fingers, as the heat can linger and linger, lying in wait for you to innocently wipe your eyes and plunging you into pain.*
The green pepper in this salsa add a pepper flavor without the heat of all the chilis. If you prefer it hotter, use 2 Anaheim or poblanos, or 3 jalapeños in place of the green pepper.

1 green pepper

1 large mild chili, such as Anaheim or poblano

2 jalapeños

3 cloves garlic, chopped

juice of ½ lime or to taste

1tsp. salt

1tbsp. olive oil

large dash oregano

large dash cumin seeds

1. Roast the green pepper and chilis under a hot broiler, in a heavy ungreased skillet or over an open flame, until they are scorched and charred. Place in a paper or plastic bag or bowl with a tightly fitted lid, and seal. Let stand for 30–45 minutes, or until they sweat their skins off. Remove the stems, seeds, and skins, then dice the flesh.

2. Combine the pepper and chilis with the garlic, lime juice, salt, and olive oil, then purée. Taste for seasoning and add the oregano and cumin seeds to taste.

NUTRITIONAL INFORMATION			
	TOTAL FAT	SAT FAT	CHOL	ENERGY
Total	12g	2g	0mg	138kcals

CHIPOTLES EN ADOBO

CONDIMENT OF SMOKED CHILIS
IN SWEET-SPICY SAUCE

6 dried chipotle chilis, cut into halves

1 large or 2 medium onions, chopped

6 cloves garlic, chopped

6tbsp. cider vinegar or to taste

6tbsp. tomato catsup

2tbsp. sugar, preferably dark sugar

dash salt

2 cups water

1tbsp. vegetable oil

large dash each allspice or cloves, cinnamon, and cumin

3–4tbsp. lime juice or combination of pineapple and lemon juice

1. Place the chipotles in a saucepan with half the onion, 5 cloves of garlic, the vinegar, catsup, sugar, salt, water, oil, and spices.

2. Bring to a boil, then simmer over a low heat for about 20 minutes or until the chilis are softened and the sauce is thickened.

3. Remove the chili mixture from the heat and add the remaining onion and garlic. Stir in the lime juice and taste for sugar, salt, and cloves, adding more to balance the flavor. Let cool. Store in the refrigerator for up to a week.

NUTRITIONAL INFORMATION			
	TOTAL FAT	SAT FAT	CHOL	ENERGY
Total	85g	19g	344mg	1520 kcals

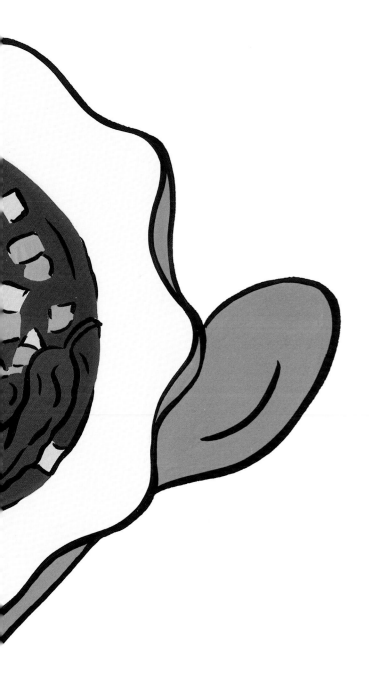

CEBOLLAS EN ESCABECHE A LA YUCATECA
PICKLED ONION RINGS
FROM THE YUCATAN

Cebollas en Escabeche are used to garnish nearly everything in the Yucatán. Their tart zing of flavor makes a perfect foil to the sultry flavors of the spicy mixtures of that region: smoky broiled vegetables, spices, seeds, and nuts, all ground into complex seasoning pastes.

2–3 red onions, peeled and thinly sliced	juice of 1 orange, plus grated rind of ¼ orange
½ cup cider vinegar	¼ cup water
juice of 2 limes	salt to taste
	dash crumbled dried oregano

1. Combine all the ingredients together. Let sit overnight. Chill until ready to use.

NUTRITIONAL INFORMATION				
	TOTAL FAT	SAT FAT	CHOL	ENERGY
Total	85g	19g	344mg	1520 kcals

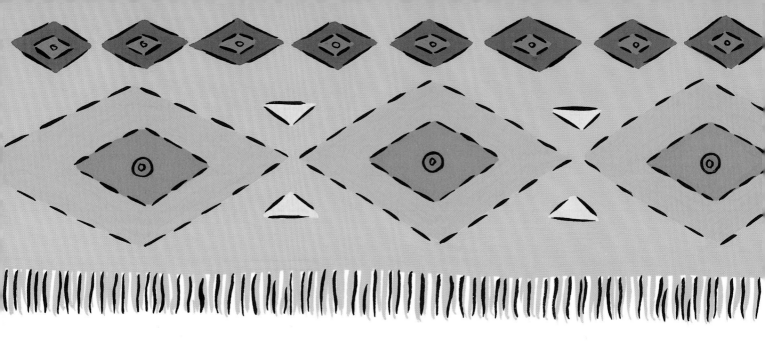

CHAPTER FIVE

BASICS

★ ★ ★ ★ ★

MEXICAN MAINSTAYS

Whether at home, in restaurants, cafés or street stalls, there are basic dishes that form the makeup of all the others: tortillas, beans, and savory mixtures of tender meats and poultry to be stuffed into antojitos.

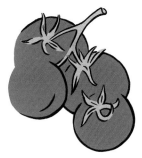

TOSTADAS

Stale tortillas make the crispest tostadas as they absorb less oil in the frying.

LOWER FAT TOSTADAS

Brush stale tortillas with vegetable oil and place on a baking sheet in the oven at 425°. Bake until golden and lightly browned in places and crisp, about 15 minutes. Alternatively, bake in the oven at 300° for 45 minutes or so. The long slow bake gives a crisper, more brittle crunch to the tostadas. Remove and place on a dry surface.

TRADITIONAL TOSTADAS

Fry the tortillas, one at a time, in shallow vegetable oil or melted lard or shortening, until crisp and golden brown. Remove from the pan and drain on paper towels, then place on a dry surface. Keep warm in the oven at 350° for up to 10 minutes: lower the heat to 275° if keeping warm for up to 1 hour.

TOTOPOS (TORTILLA CHIPS)

Cut tortillas into wedges and prepare either in method 1 or 2. Use for chilaquiles, nachos, or for tortilla soup.

TORTILLAS DE MAIZ

CORN TORTILLAS

The soft pat, pat, pat of hands slapping against each other flattening out the masa that becomes the tortilla is the traditional background music for the parade of life in much of Mexico.

Modern times have eroded it somewhat: your local taqueria is more likely to have a little machine rolling out the tender flat corn cakes than to have a woman in the kitchen grinding, patting, and cooking. But it is still there, sometimes, that elusive comforting sound.

In the city, tortillas are likely to be purchased, or made in the home with a nifty little metal tortilla press. And if the romantic patting sound is sometimes missing, the flavor of the tortillas is still marvelous: earthy, tender corn-scented flat breads, tasting like the essence of Mexican food and like nothing else.

Tortillas of course form the basis of much of Mexican cuisine: they are eaten as bread for wrapping up morsels of food, used as utensils for scooping up food, and even as the plate itself, with food placed on top.

MAKES 12 6 INCH TORTILLAS
MAKES 24 3 INCH TORTILLAS

1lb. masa flour

¾–1 cup warm room temperature water (less if weather is humid)

several plastic bags, side cut so that each forms a large rectangle

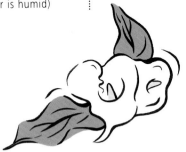

1. Mix the flour with the water until it forms a soft but not sticky dough.

2. Heat a heavy skillet or comal; I find that using two at a time makes the task quicker and is useful when serving warm tortillas with the meal.

3. Roll a piece of dough into a ball about 1½ inches in diameter. Place this ball on one side of a rectangle, then place this onto the open tortilla press. Cover with the other side of the plastic.

4. Close the press and push the handle down evenly and hard. Open up and take the tortilla out of the press – this is easiest to do by picking up the whole press carefully, then peel off the plastic and transfer the tortilla directly into the hot pan. Lightly oiling your hands makes it easier to handle the dough.

If the dough is thick and grainy, it is too dry; if it makes too-fragile tortillas that stick to either the plastic bag or the pan, it is too wet. As the dough tends to dry out as it stands (while you make the other tortillas), you will probably need to add a little more water to the dough, kneading it well as you do.

5. Cook each tortilla quickly, about 2 minutes total. When cooking the first side, wait for the edges to appear dry, then turn over and cook the second side until it is lightly speckled. Turn over and cook the first side a few more moments, then stack on a plate, and keep warm covered with a clean cloth. Tortillas may puff up as they cook; this is a good sign, indicating a light well cooked tortilla. (Some specialties, such as the Yucatecan stuffed tortilla dish, panuchos, are made with tortillas that are especially puffed.)

NUTRITIONAL INFORMATION				
	TOTAL FAT	SAT FAT	CHOL	ENERGY
Total	16.5g	0g	0mg	1840kcals
Per Serving (12)	1g	0g	0mg	153kcals
Per Serving (24)	0.5g	0g	0mg	77kcals

TORTILLAS DE HARINA

FLOUR TORTILLAS

Flour tortillas, soft flatcakes of wheatflour, are most popular in the northern state of Sonora as they are in the regions that lie north of the border: Arizona and New Mexico.

Wheat was brought here by the cowboys and herders of the Ranchos that covered the area, ground into flour, and rolled out into soft flaccid pancake-like breads rather than puffy, yeast-risen European breads.

Flour tortillas range in size from 4 inches to 14 or 20 inch rounds. The larger rounds are stuffed and rolled into burritos and chimichangas.

Note: Lard is the traditional fat used to make flour tortillas. You can buy flour tortillas made with vegetable fat or oil, or even completely fat-free. Whole wheat tortillas, oatbran tortillas, tomato, spinach, and other vegetable tortillas can sometimes be found in health food stores.

MAKES 10–12 9 INCH TORTILLAS

½ cup lard or shortening or ½ cup vegetable oil

1lb. all-purpose flour, preferably white unbleached, sifted

1 cup lukewarm water

2tsp. salt

1. Work the lard or oil into the flour with your fingers or in a food processor, until it forms a sandy, crumblike mixture.

2. Mix the water and salt, then stir into the flour.

3. Knead the dough for about 3 minutes or until it is no longer sticky. Cover and set aside for at least 2 hours or overnight.

4. Knead the dough again, then roll into small balls. For 7 inch tortillas, make 2 inch balls, 14 inch tortillas will need balls about 3 inches in diameter.

5. Place each ball on a floured board, then roll into a 7 inch round, paper thin, turning the dough so that the round becomes thin and circular.

6. Heat an ungreased heavy skillet, griddle, or comal. It should be very hot. Place a flat dough round on the hot surface. Leave it for 20–30 seconds – if it puffs up, flatten it again with the back of a spatula.

7. Turn and cook on the other side, only about 10 seconds this time. Stack onto a plate, and keep covered with a clean cloth while you prepare the rest of the dough. The tortillas should be soft and flexible.

8. To use, reheat on the griddle before filling, etc.

NUTRITIONAL INFORMATION

	TOTAL FAT	SAT FAT	CHOL	ENERGY
Total	130g	51g	116mg	2819kcals
Per Serving (10)	13g	5g	12mg	282kcals
Per Serving (12)	11g	4g	10mg	235kcals

REHEATING BOUGHT TORTILLAS, BOTH WHEAT AND CORN MASA

Tortillas should be moist and pliable when reheated. A steamer can do an excellent job, though too much water in the pan and too long cooking can end with sticky results. I prefer the following method, using a lightly oiled skillet.

1. Lightly spray each tortilla and let them sit a few minutes while you heat a heavy lightly oiled skillet.

2. Put the whole stack of tortillas in it. When the bottom tortilla is warm, turn the whole stack using a spatula, so that the bottom tortilla is now the top one, or a middle one.

3. Cover and let to cook in the steam for a few moments, then repeat, dividing the stack of tortillas from the middle. You want each tortilla to be exposed to both heat of the bottom of the pan and the steam that rises to the top.

4. Remove from the pan and place on a plate or in a clean tea cloth, sides folded over to keep the tortillas soft and warm.

FRIJOLES

BEANS

At almost any moment in most any kitchen in Mexico, simmering quietly on a back burner is the earthenware casserole known as "olla," filled with soupy bubbling beans. Such soupy, tender beans, known as frijoles de olla, accompany nearly every meal. They are also ladled into soups, served with meats, puréed and fried then served spread on tortillas for an endless array of tacos, tostadas, and enchiladas or enfrijoladas. The liquid from cooking beans is used in soups and stews, and to cook rice. (Arroz negro, rice cooked in black bean liquor is startlingly gray in color but so very savory and satisfying to eat.)
The color, size and shape of your beans depends on where in Mexico you are. In general, black beans are eaten in the Southern more tropical regions, pink and pinto beans further north. However, within this oversimplification there is a huge spectrum of beans and their dishes. White beans, garbanzo beans, lima beans, yellow beans, all are doted on, added to soups and simmered meals of meats and vegetables.

FRIJOLES REFRITOS

"REFRIED" BEANS

Despite the name "refried", frijoles refritos is not fried twice, rather it is puréed and heated in a small amount of hot fat, more or less fried once. I have heard it said that it is with typical South of the Border exuberance that many things are exaggerated, even the times the beans are fried.

SERVES 6 – 8

1 recipe pinto, pinquito or other pink beans from Frijoles de Olla (page 77)

1–2 onions, chopped

3tbsp. vegetable oil

½tsp. ground cumin

½tsp. mild chili powder

salt to taste

1. Mash or purée the beans to obtain a coarse chunky consistency. Leave some whole, some in pieces, others puréed into a thick saucelike mixture.
2. Sauté the onion in the vegetable oil until softened and lightly browned, then sprinkle in the cumin and chili powder.

3. Ladle in a scoop of the bean mixture. Cook over medium high heat until thickened and slightly darkened in color. Add another ladleful of the beans and repeat until all the beans have simmered into a thick, darkened, flavorful mixture.
4. Season with salt to taste.

NUTRITIONAL INFORMATION			
	TOTAL FAT	SAT FAT	CHOL	ENERGY
Total	60g	13g	45mg	2347kcals
Per Serving (6)	10g	2g	8mg	391kcals
Per Serving (8)	7.5g	1.5g	6mg	293kcals

VARIATION
FRIJOLES REFRITOS CON QUESO

Top refried pinto or other pink beans with about 1½ cups shredded mild white cheese and either heat in the oven or stir in. Let the cheese melt, then serve.

SIMMERED BEANS

The green herb epazote, said to help mitigate the embarrassing effects of beans, is usually added to the pot of simmering beans. If unavailable fresh, sometimes it can be found dried. A leaf or two of mint, while not the same thing, gives a similar flavor and result.

Use these beans as an accompaniment to make frijoles refritos, or anywhere it calls for simmered beans. A bowl of warm frijoles de olla, along with a few warm tortillas and a chili or two is the mainstay of the Mexican diet.

Any of the speckled, most unusual beans such as the earthy, rich Anasazi, are especially delicious cooked this way.

SERVES 6-8

1lb. pinto (or pinquito, or pink) or black beans, picked over for stones etc, soaked	1 head of garlic, unpeeled and cut into halves crosswise
2 medium onions, chopped	8oz. smoky bacon
	3 sprigs of epazote or several leaves of mint
	salt to taste

1. Soak the beans overnight or do a quick soak: place the beans in a saucepan with cold water to cover. Bring to a boil, cook for a few minutes, then remove from the heat. Let sit, covered, for an hour. The beans should have plumped up and softened somewhat, absorbing water in the process.

2. Add the onion, garlic, bacon, epazote or mint, and water to the pan.

3. Bring to a boil, then reduce the heat to low and simmer, uncovered, stirring once or twice, for 1½–2 hours or until the beans are softened.

4. Add salt to taste.

NUTRITIONAL INFORMATION				
	TOTAL FAT	SAT FAT	CHOL	ENERGY
Total	27g	9g	45mg	2005kcals
Per Serving (6)	4.5g	1.5g	8mg	334kcals
Per Serving (8)	3g	1g	6mg	251kcals

COOKED TOMATO SAUCE

This all-purpose tomato and pepper sauce can be used to top eggs for Huevos Rancheros (page 62), served with broiled fish and plantains, thinned with stock for soup. The recipe makes about 4½ pints and keeps in the refrigerator up to a week, in the freezer for up to 2 months (though it will pale when reheated and needs to be spiced up with chili pepper upon thawing).

2tsp. cumin seeds	2–3 small hot dried chilis, crumbled, or 1 large mild green chili, such as poblano, roasted, peeled, and diced
3lb. tomatoes, diced (canned is fine)	
⅓ cup vegetable oil	1 green pepper, roasted, peeled, and diced
2–3 small to medium onions, chopped	salt to taste
4–6 cloves, garlic, chopped	2–4tbsp. chopped fresh cilantro (optional)
1tbsp. oregano, crumbled	

1. Toast the cumin seeds until fragrant, then crush coarsely. Set aside.

2. Purée the tomatoes and set aside.

3. Sauté the onions and garlic in the oil until softened, then add the cumin, the oregano, chili, green pepper, and puréed tomatoes.

4. Simmer, stirring often for about 45 minutes or until the sauce is richly flavored and thickened. Season with salt to taste, adding cilantro if using.

NUTRITIONAL INFORMATION			
	TOTAL FAT	SAT FAT	CHOL	ENERGY
Total	96g	12.5g	0mg	1162kcals

SALSA DE CHILE PASILLA

MILD RED CHILI SAUCE

This is the classic red chili sauce for making enchiladas, or simmering meats, or for spicing up soups or braises. You can omit the tomatoes if you like; or use stock for soaking the chilis for a richer-flavored sauce.

Add this sauce to browned beef or pork as the braising liquid. Simmer until tender for an excellent chili rojo con carne, to spoon into bowls or wrap into tortillas for burritos and tacos.

SERVES 4

4 large dried chilis, either all pasilla or half ancho and half pasilla	¼tsp. ground cumin
about 2 cups hot but not boiling water or stock	dash ground cinnamon
	dash thyme
6 cloves garlic, unpeeled	2–3tsp. sugar
1 onion, peeled	salt to taste
1 clove garlic, chopped	1tbsp. vegetable oil
6 ripe tomatoes, quartered (14oz.)	juice of ½ lime, plus more if needed to taste

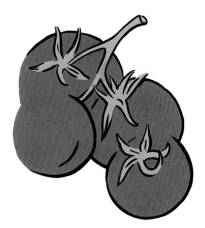

1. Lightly toast the chilis over an open flame or in a heavy ungreased skillet until they change color.

2. Remove the stems, seeds, and veins from the chilis. Break up into little pieces and place in a bowl or saucepan. Leave, covered, with a lid, to soften for about 20 minutes. (The liquid should be cool enough to touch and the chilis softened and fleshy.)

3. Meanwhile, roast the whole garlic cloves and onion chunks in an ungreased pan until lightly charred and the garlic is tender. Remove from the heat. When cool enough to handle, remove the skins from the garlic.

4. Chop the garlic and onion and place in a blender with the raw chopped garlic, tomatoes, chilis, and enough of the soaking liquid to make a smoothish sauce. When the sauce is smooth, blend in the rest of the soaking liquid and season with cumin, cinnamon, thyme, sugar, and salt. (The sauce may be sieved for a smoother, more digestible texture.)

5. Heat the vegetable oil until hot, then ladle in about half of the chili sauce. Cook down for a few minutes, then ladle in the rest. Cook for about 10 minutes or until the sauce thickens a little and concentrates its flavor.

6. Remove from the heat and season with lime, spices, salt, and sugar.

NUTRITIONAL INFORMATION				
	TOTAL FAT	SAT FAT	CHOL	ENERGY
Total	13.5g	2g	0mg	323kcals
Per Serving	3g	0.5g	0mg	81kcals

VARIATIONS
USING DIFFERENT CHILIS

All mild chili sauces can be prepared this way. For guajillo salsa, use guajillo chilis. Cascabel salsa, use cascabel chilis. Chilis such as ancho, negro, mulatto, and some pasillas, will give a dark, almost chocolatey sauce. Light red chilis, such as New Mexico, California, guajillo, and some pasilla, will give a brighter lighter red colored sauce with a lighter, brighter flavor.

MEAT AND POULTRY FILLINGS

Any chili-scented Mexican spiced mixture makes an excellent filling for tacos,
tostadas, burritos, and the like. Leftover barbecued chicken or fish, pieces of
braised ancho-seasoned pot roast, shreds of meat left over from a braised dinner;
all of these make delicious antojito fillings.

CARNE PARA TACOS
SIMMERED PORK FILLING

S E R V E S   4

2lb. boneless pork, with a little fat for flavor, cut into large bite-sized chunks	1 onion, coarsely chopped
any bones cut from the joint	2 cloves garlic, whole and peeled
	salt and pepper to taste

1. Place the meat in a saucepan with the bones, onion, garlic, salt, and pepper.

2. Add cold water to reach the top of the pan. Bring to a boil, then lower the heat and simmer over a very low heat until the meat is just tender, about 1 hour. Remove from the heat and let meat cool in its stock.

3. Take the meat from the stock (save the stock for soup). Shred the meat with a fork and taste for salt and pepper. Warm or brown as desired.

NUTRITIONAL INFORMATION			
	TOTAL FAT	SAT FAT	CHOL	ENERGY
Total	71g	25g	690mg	1512kcals

V A R I A T I O N S
CARNITAS

Add ¼tsp. oregano to the meat and add just enough water to cover the meat but no more. Simmer uncovered until the meat is tender and liquid has evaporated. The meat should begin to brown as the liquid reduces and the fat from the meat is rendered out. Continue cooking as the meat browns; turn occasionally and sprinkle with a dash of cumin as it cooks. Season with salt and pepper to taste and cook until the meat is very tender and nicely browned. This is easily done in the oven as well, instead of the top of the stove.

CARNE DE RES PARA TACOS (BEEF FILLING)

In place of pork in the previous recipe use beef, choosing a cut that has enough fat to encourage browning. If using a lean cut of beef, brown it in a nonstick skillet with a tiny amount of olive oil to encourage a crusty brown result.

POLLO DESHEBBRADO
SIMMERED CHICKEN

This makes a basic poached chicken that can be used for tacos, tostadas, and salads. The cooking liquid makes excellent stock.

S E R V E S   4

1 chicken, about 3lb.	1 onion, chopped
chicken stock to cover (or water mixed with a bouillon cube or two)	large dash oregano
	salt and pepper to taste

1. Combine all the ingredients in a saucepan and bring to a boil. Reduce the heat and simmer over a very low heat for 1 hour and 20 minutes or until chicken is just cooked through.

2. Let chicken cool in its liquid, then remove from the pan (saving the delicious liquid for soup or sauce). Dice or pull apart the meat with your fingers.

3. Season with salt and pepper to taste.

NUTRITIONAL INFORMATION			
	TOTAL FAT	SAT FAT	CHOL	ENERGY
Total	45g	13g	630mg	1250kcals/5262kJ

INDEX

Index compiled by Sheila Seacroft